YO-YO MA

YO-YO MA

A Biography

Jim Whiting

GREENWOOD BIOGRAPHIES

GREENWOOD PRESS
WESTPORT, CONNECTICUT • LONDON

Library of Congress Cataloging-in-Publication Data

Whiting, Jim, 1943–
Yo-Yo Ma : a biography / Jim Whiting.
   p. cm. — (Greenwood biographies, ISSN 1540–4900)
   Includes bibliographical references and index.
   ISBN 978–0–313–34486–2 (alk. paper)
   1. Ma, Yo-Yo, 1955–   2. Violoncellists—Biography.   I. Title.
   ML418.M115W55   2008
   787.4092—dc22
   [B]   2008017546

British Library Cataloguing in Publication Data is available

Library of Congress Catalog Card Number: 200817546

ISBN: 978–0–313–34486–2
ISSN: 1540–4900

First published in 2008

Greenwood Press, 88 Post Road West, Westport, CT 06881
An imprint of Greenwood Publishing Group, Inc.
www.greenwood.com

Printed in the United States of America

The paper used in this book complies with the
Permanent Paper Standard issued by the National
Information Standards Organization (Z39.48–1984).

10   9   8   7   6   5   4   3   2   1

CONTENTS

vi					CONTENTS

Photo essay follows page 88

SERIES FOREWORD

In response to high school and public library needs, Greenwood developed this distinguished series of full-length biographies specifically for student use. Prepared by field experts and professionals, these engaging biographies are tailored for high school students who need challenging yet accessible biographies. Ideal for secondary school assignments, the length, format, and subject areas are designed to meet educators' requirements and students' interests.

Greenwood offers an extensive selection of biographies spanning all curriculum-related subject areas including social studies, the sciences, literature and the arts, history and politics, as well as popular culture, covering public figures and famous personalities from all time periods and backgrounds, both historic and contemporary, who have made an impact on American and/or world culture. Greenwood biographies were chosen based on comprehensive feedback from librarians and educators. Consideration was given to both curriculum relevance and inherent interest. The result is an intriguing mix of the well known and the unexpected, the saints and sinners from long-ago history and contemporary pop culture. Readers will find a wide array of subject choices from fascinating crime figures like Al Capone to inspiring pioneers like Margaret Mead, from the greatest minds of our time like Stephen Hawking to the most amazing success stories of our day like J. K. Rowling.

While the emphasis is on fact, not glorification, the books are meant to be fun to read. Each volume provides in-depth information about the subject's life from birth through childhood, the teen years, and adulthood. A thorough account relates family background and education, traces

personal and professional influences, and explores struggles, accomplishments, and contributions. A timeline highlights the most significant life
events against a historical perspective. Bibliographies supplement the reference value of each volume.

INTRODUCTION

As the final notes of the opening selection fade away, the audience at Seattle's Benaroya Hall applauds enthusiastically. Moments later, one of the musicians strides to the front of the stage and addresses the capacity throng, providing background to what they have just heard—as well he might.

Benaroya Hall is the home venue of the Seattle Symphony Orchestra. It normally features music by such well-known classical composers as Ludwig van Beethoven, Johann Sebastian Bach, and Wolfgang Amadeus Mozart. But on this night—March 12, 2007—few in the audience have heard any of the music that is on the program. Nor are they familiar with any of the composers' names.

There is another difference between this performance and the ones to which most members of the audience are accustomed. A normal concert at Benaroya Hall would present grand orchestral works played by nearly 100 black-clad musicians. The orchestra members would be sitting in hard-backed chairs arranged in precise rows. In contrast, tonight's group has barely a dozen performers. Most are dressed casually and a few even sit cross-legged on a large platform in the center of the stage.

These musicians are known as the Silk Road Ensemble. Having been formed in 1998, less than 10 years before this night's concert, the ensemble is a relatively new group, and relative to the world of classical music, its members have a new goal: to bridge the musical gap between East and West.

Tonight it seems evident, after playing just one selection, that they have achieved their goal. The response to their piece is not the polite clapping of a classical music audience hearing compositions in which they are not truly interested. Instead, the applause is enthusiastic. The listeners are obviously in a good mood. When the musician concludes his introductory words by saying, "Here's another musician to explain what you're about to hear next," they chuckle.

The man who buoyantly strides to the front of the stage is hardly "another musician." In fact, he is the primary reason why this performance and a similar one the following evening have been sold out for months. He is cellist Yo-Yo Ma, the world's best-known classical musician.

Fifteen Grammy awards and scores of best-selling recordings attest to Yo-Yo Ma's professional success. His popularity extends far beyond the confines of classical music. For example, an issue of *People* magazine in 2001 named him one of the "50 Sexiest Men Alive." In 2004, another publication went even further. "If you were an alien tasked to bring home earth's most charming male, Yo-Yo Ma would head up your short list,"[1] it said.

Yet in another way, the description of Yo-Yo Ma as "another musician" is completely accurate. Many famous musicians—whether they are pop stars or classical artists—jealously insist on continually being in the spotlight and are reluctant to share their glory. Not Yo-Yo. As he shows the audience tonight, he is content to blend into the ensemble.

For some audience members, Yo-Yo's low visibility is a letdown. "I'm really disappointed," one of them grumps during the intermission. "I hoped for a little more Yo-Yo." It's unlikely that the rest of the evening is an improvement from his point of view. When the published program ends, an immediate and sustained standing ovation generates several encores. Many patrons hope that Yo-Yo will take his cello, sit by himself in the front of the stage, and play. Instead, he deflects the attention to other members of the ensemble, allowing them to demonstrate their own considerable ability.

This lack of self-glorification is consistent with his goal in founding the Silk Road Ensemble. He isn't trying to use it to advance his own very well-established career. Instead, he wants to help create international understanding by crossing musical boundaries. He is convinced that although people speak different languages, they can all understand music, regardless of the nationality of the composer.

NOTE

1. "Yo-Yo Ma: Earth's Most Charming Male?" *Goldsea Asian American Daily,* May 26, 2004, http://goldsea.com/Air/Issues/Ma/ma.html.

TIMELINE: EVENTS IN THE LIFE OF YO-YO MA

1911	Hiao-Tsiun Ma, his father, born in Ningbo, China.
1923	Ya-Wen Lo, his mother, born in Hong Kong.
1949	Parents marry on July 17; mother changes her name to Marina Ma.
1951	Sister Yeou-Cheng born on July 28.
1955	Yo-Yo Ma born in Paris on October 7.
1959	At age 3, Yo-Yo decides to play cello.
1961	Plays first recital, at Institute of Art and Archaeology in Paris, accompanied by Yeou-Cheng.
1962	Moves with family to New York City; studies with Janos Scholz; auditions for Pablo Casals; performs with sister and Leonard Bernstein at the American Pageant of the Arts on November 29.
1964	Begins studying with Leonard Rose.
1968	Enters Professional Children's School; appears with San Francisco Little Symphony.
1971	Gives recital at Carnegie Hall; graduates from Professional Children's School; enrolls at Columbia but soon drops out; attends Meadowmount summer camp.
1972	Attends Marlboro Music Festival; meets Jill Hornor; enters Harvard.
1975	Begins playing with pianist Emanuel Ax.
1976	Graduates from Harvard.

1978   Marries Jill Hornor; wins Avery Fisher Prize.

1980   Undergoes spine operation.

1983   Birth of son Nicholas; acquires 1733 Domenico Montagnana and "Davidov" Stradivari cellos.

1984   Wins first Grammy, for Bach cello suites; death of Leonard Rose.

1985   Daughter Emily is born; wins two Grammys.

1987   Given opportunity to purchase Davidov cello but declines; an anonymous patron purchases it and provides it for him for the rest of his playing career.

1989   Records *Anything Goes* with Stéphane Grappelli.

1991   Receives honorary doctorate from Harvard; father Hiao-Tsiun dies.

1992   Records *Hush* with Bobby McFerrin.

1993   Visits Kalahari Bushmen.

1996   Releases *Appalachia Waltz* with Edgar Meyer and Mark O'Connor.

1997   Releases *Soul of the Tango*, which wins Grammy as Best Classical Crossover album.

1998   *Inspired by Bach* premieres on PBS; founds Silk Road Project.

1999   Forgets Montagnana cello in a New York City cab, though he quickly recovers it.

2000   Releases soundtrack of *Crouching Tiger, Hidden Dragon*.

2001   Performs with violinist Itzhak Perlman at Academy Awards; Silk Road Ensemble begins first tour.

2002   Performs during opening ceremonies of Winter Olympics in Salt Lake City.

2003   Releases *Obrigado Brazil*, which becomes his 15th Grammy winner.

2004   Receives Harvard Arts Medal.

2006   Wins $1 million Dan David Prize for "cultural heritage protection" through the Silk Road Project; named United Nations Messenger of Peace.

2007   Opens Seattle Symphony and New York Philharmonic seasons; visits China.

2008   Receives Crystal Award from the World Economic Forum.

Chapter 1

LOVE AND WAR

Although the Silk Road Ensemble represents Yo-Yo Ma's highest-profile effort to create international understanding through music, his career, which spans several decades, reflects many similar endeavors. In light of all of these contributions, in September 2006 Yo-Yo Ma was named a member of the United Nations Messengers of Peace—one of the most exclusive groups on earth.

According to the Web site of the Spokesperson for the Secretary General of the United Nations, "United Nations Messengers of Peace are individuals who possess widely recognized talents in the fields of arts, literature, music and sports and who have agreed to help focus world-wide attention on the work of the United Nations."[1]

At the time of Yo-Yo's appointment, there were just nine other Messengers of Peace: boxing great Muhammad Ali, tennis player Vijay Amritraj, author and journalist Anna Cataldi, actor and producer Michael Douglas, primate expert Jane Goodall, singer and composer Enrico Macias, jazz musician Wynton Marsalis, opera singer Luciano Pavarotti, and Nobel Peace Prize–winning author Elie Wiesel. (Within two years, the list would add actor George Clooney, conductor Daniel Barenboim, author Paulo Coelho, violinist Midori Goto, and Olympic equestrian competitor Princess Haya of Jordan.)

At the ceremony marking Yo-Yo's appointment, which included him playing a composition for solo cello written by Turkish composer Ahmed Adnan Saygun, then-U.N. Secretary-General Kofi Annan remarked, "Over the course of your extraordinary musical career, you have demonstrated time and again your dedication to overcoming cultural differences and bridging gaps between nations and generations. . . . Through your music, the message of peace can spread far and wide and influence people around the world to focus on harmony and human dignity."[2]

In light of Yo-Yo's long and well-documented emphasis on peace, it is ironic that he almost certainly owes his birth to the circumstances of war.

His father, Hiao-Tsiun Ma, was born in July 1911 in Ningbo, a city located near the coast of central China about 100 miles south of Shanghai. His family was reasonably well off and encouraged him to pursue his early interest in music, which included learning to play the violin and composing. He attended the National Central University, located in Nanking (which is sometimes spelled Nanjing), about 200 miles northwest of Ningbo. At the time, the city was the capital of China.

After graduation, Hiao-Tsiun remained at the university and taught music theory and other courses. Under normal circumstances, it is likely that he would have spent the rest of his life there, working with successive generations of students and conveying his love of music to them.

But the circumstances in China at this time were far from normal. For nearly 4,000 years, the country had been ruled by a series of dynasties, in which emperors had passed on their power to family members. In the decades before Hiao-Tsiun's birth, the power of these emperors had been declining and many Chinese wanted a different form of government that would include the participation of common people.

Barely two months after Hiao-Tsiun's birth, this situation came to a head when police fired on demonstrators in the remote Sichuan Province. That outburst kindled a rebellion that soon spread throughout China, and early in 1912, when Hiao-Tsiun was a few months old, the Republic of China came into existence. However, the new government was weak. For years China was fragmented as armies that owed their allegiance to warlords fought among each other. In the mid-1920s, the Kuomintang Party, under the leadership of Chiang Kai-Shek, defeated the warlords and unified China. Soon afterward, Chiang attacked the Chinese Communist Party, which formerly had been a part of the Kuomintang. Hiao-Tsiun grew up in the resulting civil war, which began in 1927 and didn't end until 1949.

The situation became even more complicated in 1931 when the increasingly powerful Japanese invaded the northern Chinese province of Manchuria and installed a puppet government. It was soon evident that the Japanese wanted more Chinese territory. Amid raging civil war and the threat of Japanese incursions into other parts of China, Hiao-Tsiun left his homeland in 1936 at age 25 to continue his musical studies in Paris.

The decision may well have saved his life. In July of 1937, Japan invaded mainland China. Nanking was one of the primary targets. Japanese troops overcame minimal resistance and captured the city in mid-December. For the next month and a half, what became known as the Rape of Nanking took place. Hundreds of thousands of Chinese, most of whom were civilians, perished. Some drowned trying to escape. Many were shot. Others were bayoneted, beheaded, or buried alive. Thousands of women were assaulted.

The university was a special target. As *Time* magazine observed in 1940:

> China's university men monopolized Government offices, ruled China's millions. Active, patriotic, brave, they were the hope of the New China.
>
> First victims of Japan's invasion in the summer of 1937 were China's universities. Concentrated along the coast, in Peking, Tientsin, Shanghai, Nanking, Hong Kong, Canton, they were at once Japan's most dangerous foes and easiest targets. Japanese bombs completely destroyed Nankai University in Tientsin; not a book or piece of equipment was saved. Japanese soldiers looted National Peking University, sold its furniture for cigaret money. At Tsing Hua University, in Peking, Japanese smashed laboratories to bits, converted the Theodore Roosevelt Memorial Gymnasium into a stable, the John Hay Memorial Library into a hospital.[3]

National Central University was bombed four times in rapid succession before the city was captured. It is sobering to note that it did not fare as poorly as some of its fellow schools. However, it plainly would not last long once the Japanese entered the city. Students and teachers packed as much property as they could onto small boats and spent several weeks voyaging up the Yangtze River to Chungking, more than a thousand miles away. Anyone connected with the university who didn't escape almost certainly perished.

Hiao-Tsiun in Paris was thousands of miles from the violence that had engulfed his native land, but he soon found himself in the center of another conflict. The German Army invaded Poland in September of 1939 and launched World War II. The following May, German troops entered Paris. The German occupation of the City of Light was not nearly as bloody as the Japanese occupation of Nanking. Still, living under foreign domination was not easy for Hiao-Tsiun.

"During the German occupation of Paris, my father lived by himself in a garret," Yo-Yo later said. "He would memorize violin pieces by Bach and play them in the dark."[4]

Though France and indeed the world were embroiled in war, Hiao-Tsiun managed to return to his teaching position at National Central University. It had successfully relocated to Chungking, hundreds of miles away from the invading Japanese. But Hiao-Tsiun's tenure there was *not* successful. As one of his students much later observed:

> Students at the University had no heart to apply themselves seriously to intellectual pursuits. Mentally stressed out, they did not measure up to Dr. Ma's exacting standards. He could well understand, empathize and sympathize with them, but what he could not tolerate was their indifference toward their school work. For him, a perfectionist, there was no excuse for not fulfilling one's responsibilities. Instead of allowing his students to wallow in pessimism, he exhorted them to redouble their efforts in the face of adversity. . . . His exhortations, nevertheless, fell on deaf ears.[5]

However, no one could say that the student who made this observation had "deaf ears." Her name was Ya-Wen Lo, and her presence at the university was directly connected with the war.

She had been born in 1923 in Hong Kong, an island just off the southern Chinese coast that had been a British colony since 1841. Her family raised her there, but their peaceful life could not last. The Japanese attacked Hong Kong on December 7, 1941, a few hours after their assault on the U.S. naval base at Pearl Harbor, Hawaii. On Christmas Day of 1941, after 18 days of fighting, Hong Kong fell. Ya-Wen's father, a prosperous rice merchant, feared for her safety under Japanese occupation. He sent her to a boarding school on the mainland to complete her final year of high school. Ya-Wen's family was close-knit and she was unhappy at the separation. She consoled herself with the knowledge that she would return home when the school year was over.

Her hopes were short-lived. Hong Kong was no safer in 1942 than it had been when she left. For her education to continue, she had to find a safe place. The place chosen was National Central University, several hundred miles from the furthest Japanese penetration into the interior.

Though she was now even further from home, Ya-Wen immersed herself in her studies. She knew that she wanted to become an opera singer. The university offered a number of music courses that suited her perfectly.

One of them was music theory. Her professor was Hiao-Tsiun Ma. Soon she realized that there was more to her enjoyment of the class than learning the information that Hiao-Tsiun was conveying. She was developing a crush on him.

Fortunately for her, she had a friend in whom she could confide. This was none other than Tsiun-Cheng Ma—her professor's sister. Tsiun-Cheng realized that Ya-Wen was interested in her brother as a person and quickly assured her that he wasn't romantically involved with anyone else. But Ya-Wen's chance for a relationship with Hiao-Tsiun disappeared when, unhappy with the performance of his students, he decided to return to Paris and further his own studies. There he eventually earned his doctorate degree and became Dr. Hiao-Tsiun Ma.

He wasn't the only one on the move. Ya-Wen wanted to return home to Hong Kong. She was determined to find some way of studying there. She assured Tsiun-Cheng that this return was likely to be temporary, because she, Ya-Wen, wanted to go to Paris. To her good fortune, Tsiun-Cheng told her that she had the same goal. The two young women promised each other that one day they would make the trip together.

In the meantime, they needed to complete their schooling and earn enough money to make the long trip. It wasn't easy. At one point, Ya-Wen had to travel 850 miles to Shanghai to find work.

Eventually Ya-Wen realized her goal. She traveled to Paris (most likely around 1948, although the exact year is not known) and was able to take classes with Hiao-Tsiun. She realized that he was very disciplined and strict. But she also realized that their mutual love and passion for music was even stronger.

The couple was married in Paris on July 17, 1949. Upon her marriage, Ya-Wen changed her name to Marina Ma. She began further voice training and graduated from the prestigious École César Franck.

As a budding opera singer, Marina was doubtless familiar with one of the world's most famous operas, Giacomo Puccini's *La Bohème*. It details the struggles of a group of starving artists in Paris who have so little money that at one point one member of the group, an author, burns the pages of the book he is writing to provide heat in their tiny apartment.

The Mas were experiencing a similar situation in postwar Paris. Times were tough in France. Hiao-Tsiun worked hard but didn't make much money. The couple lived in a tiny, cold, one-room apartment. They continued to struggle, day after day, month after month.

Two years into their marriage, on July 25, 1951, they had their first child, a daughter. To this new little girl they gave both a French name, Marie-Thérèse, and also a traditional Chinese name. Chinese tradition calls for families to plan the names of its children several generations ahead. Under this system, the name of every member of a particular generation shares the same written character. In the Mas' case, that meant that their daughter would be named Yeou-Cheng. Yeou is the female version of the chosen character, which means "friendly."

It was also a part of Chinese tradition that the family name should precede the given name: Ma Yeou-Cheng. Placing the family name first reflected the structure of Chinese society, in which the family was the basic unit and one's family name became his or her primary identity. "If the youngster goes significantly against the system he brings shame on the family,"[6] Yo-Yo Ma said many years later.

It didn't take long for Yeou-Cheng to demonstrate that she had inherited her parents' musical ability. When she was two and a half years old, her father began giving her violin lessons. He added the piano when she turned three. The Mas' financial resources were limited. They were fortunate enough to find a piano teacher who understood the family's situation and taught the gifted little girl for free.

Yeou-Cheng's birth had presented Marina with a dilemma. Should she continue her singing career, or devote herself to being a full-time mother? In reality, she didn't have much choice. Though she and her husband were living in France, they were still heavily influenced by the Chinese traditions under which they had been raised and which went back many centuries. One of these traditions was that mothers stayed with their children. Marina accepted it.

By now, Hiao-Tsiun's mother had followed them to Paris. She brought with her an even stronger heritage of tradition; for example, she had been raised in an era when foot-binding was still prevalent. This painful procedure—which may have affected up to a billion Chinese women over a period of many centuries—began when girls were only four or five. At this young age their bones were still malleable. Their toes were deliberately broken and tightly bound, forcing them back as close to the heel as possible. The result was a foot that in adults was only three or four inches long. Walking for more than a few minutes was very painful. Marina, too, might have had her feet bound had not the new Republic of China officially abolished foot binding some 10 years before her birth. The republic's decision, coupled with the fact that girls in Hong Kong were less likely to have their feet bound than girls in mainland China, meant Marina was spared the painful procedure.

Though Hiao-Tsiun's mother now lived with her son and daughter-in-law in Paris she still subscribed to the traditional belief that Chinese women should have several children, about two years apart. By the time that her granddaughter was three, she began pressuring Marina to have another child in spite of the family's financial hardships. She especially wanted a boy, to carry on the Ma family name.

She wasn't the only source of pressure. Yeou-Cheng's piano teacher also urged Marina to have another baby. This teacher thought it was very likely that another Ma child would have the same talent as Yeou-Cheng had already shown. When Marina asked where they would put the child in their already cramped living quarters, the teacher jokingly replied that there was plenty of room on top of the piano.

Soon a third voice joined the chorus in favor of tradition. This one was decisive. Hiao-Tsiun listened to his mother and the music teacher and decided that they were right. As a traditional Chinese man, he was especially interested in having a son. While he knew that another child would strain their meager resources even further, he assured Marina that somehow they would manage.

So on October 7, 1955, Ernest Ma came into the world.

NOTES

1. "United Nations Messengers of Peace," UN Web Services Section, Department of Public Information, United Nations, 2007, http://www.un.org/News/ossg/factmess.htm.

2. "Annan Appoints Cellist Yo-Yo Ma as UN Peace Messenger for His Music of Harmony," http://www.un.org/apps/news/story.asp?NewsID=19941&Cr=messenger&Cr1=peace.

3. "Civilization's Retreat," *Time*, May 27, 1940, http://www.time.com/time/magazine/article/0,9171,884112,00.html

4. David Blum, *Quintet: Five Journeys Toward Musical Fulfillment* (Ithaca, N.Y.: Cornell University Press, 1999), p. 27.

5. Marina Ma, as told to John A. Rallo, *My Son, Yo-Yo* (Hong Kong: The Chinese University Press, 1995), p. 47.

6. Blum, *Quintet*, p. 7.

Chapter 2

"I WANT THE BIG INSTRUMENT"

In reality, the little boy had to wait a month before he received his name. That was a result of still another Chinese tradition.

"In China, there was such a great infant mortality rate that often parents would not name their child until he was one month old, because often children didn't survive that long and you didn't want to give a name and then you've bonded with your child, and then your child dies," Yo-Yo explained many years later. "So they waited, which is the Chinese way of naming the child, until November 7, which fell on the day of Saint Ernest. And so that was why I was given that French name."[1]

In view of the way that the infant would develop, this name could hardly have been less appropriate. For one thing, St. Ernest is one of the most obscure saints of the Catholic Church. No one would ever accuse Yo-Yo Ma, even as a toddler, of being "obscure." For another, St. Ernest participated in one of the Crusades, the religious wars that took place between the eleventh and thirteenth centuries. He was captured by Moors (Islamic adherents from the Iberian Peninsula and Northern Africa) and tortured to death—a mission and a fate that are both a far cry from the message of international understanding that Yo-Yo has promoted.

In accordance with long-standing family tradition, little Ernest also received the Chinese name of Yo—the male form of "friendly." He still needed a middle name.

"With me they [his parents] seem to have got lazy and been unable to think of anything else, so they added another Yo,"[2] he joked several decades later.

According to family friend John Rallo, the real reason was somewhat different. Yo "did not sound musical enough to the Mas' ears, so they added another 'Yo' rendering the name more melodious. 'Yo-Yo' rolled more easily on the tongue,"[3] he explained.

Unlike *Ernest*, this name turned out to be especially appropriate. Yo-Yo literally means "friendly friendly," and virtually everyone who comes in contact with Yo-Yo has commented about how warm and welcoming he is. Journalist Edith Eisler is typical: "When I tell people that I interviewed Yo-Yo Ma, they all ask the same question: 'Is he really as nice as he seems?' The answer is: 'No, much nicer.'"[4]

Writer Joshua Kosman adds that Yo-Yo is "the nicest person in the classical music business. . . . His personal warmth and generosity inform his playing, making every performance a richly human interaction with his listeners."[5]

His "richly human interaction" extends beyond the classical music business. In 1994, he was in Beaverton, Oregon, to film a commercial for shoe company giant Nike.

"I meet people all the time," said Kassia Sing, who was coordinating the shoot. "I just knew he was a special person. He didn't have the same ego as a lot of other people. There was a pureness of spirit with him, which was unexpected from someone of his stature."[6] During a break in the filming, Yo-Yo treated the crew to an impromptu private concert. "You could have heard a pin drop," Sing said.[7]

According to Sing, even the ride back out to the airport from the filming location was memorable. Five people crowded into the car. Any other international performing star might have chosen to stretch out comfortably in the front passenger seat. Yo-Yo was different.

"It was almost like kids arguing," Sing recalled. "He kept insisting, 'I want to sit on the hump [in the center backseat]. I like to see everything.'"[8]

His generosity of spirit has also been apparent on the occasions when he isn't the center of attention in a concert hall or a group of admirers. In 1999, Gert Kirchner, the wife of Leon Kirchner, one of Yo-Yo's music professors while he was a student at Harvard University, was lying terminally ill in a hospital. Yo-Yo came to her bedside and played his cello for her, seeking to boost her spirits. His playing seemed to help, so he returned on another occasion. As Kirchner tells the story, "Gert, who had been having an astonishing penchant for pickles, was not quite there. So I said, 'Gert, Yo-Yo is here. Do you want pickles or do you want Yo-Yo?' She said, 'I want pickles.'"[9]

Many—if not most—people with a reputation as towering as Yo-Yo's might well have taken a preference for pickles as a personal affront and stalked away. Not Yo-Yo.

"The next thing I knew, Yo-Yo left his cello and took off," Kirchner continued. "He came back about 30 minutes later with about six jars of pickles, all different kinds."[10]

Evan Eisenberg, a journalist and a college classmate of Yo-Yo's, observed that, "When a childhood friend of his (whom we both knew in college) was melancholy, he would take up his cello and play Bach for her, like David twanging arrows of song at the demons of Saul."[11]

The infant Yo-Yo nearly didn't have the chance to live up to his name and collect these glowing accolades. The Parisian winter that immediately followed his birth was one of the coldest on record. The Mas' room had no heat. Dr. Ma added more students to his teaching load to earn extra money so he could rent a hotel room for his wife and baby son. He thought the hotel room would be warmer than the apartment, where he remained with Yeou-Cheng.

But the hotel wasn't warmer. After the end of World War II, the French had made an increasingly futile attempt to hold on to Indochina, their colony in southeast Asia. Under the leadership of the charismatic Ho Chi Minh, rebel forces defeated the French army late in 1954. As the war in Indochina wound down, another one in Algeria began heating up. Algeria was across the Mediterranean Sea from France, in North Africa, but it was officially regarded as part of France, and sentiment for maintaining French control there was widespread. The high monetary cost of the conflicts in Indochina and Algeria, coupled with the lingering effects of World War II, put a severe strain on the French economy.

As was the case with many French businesses, the hotel where Marina had gone with her baby was having trouble making ends meet. To save money, its managers turned off the heat at night. The temperatures inside the building plummeted. One night Marina woke up in a state of panic. She sensed that something was wrong with Yo-Yo. When she touched him, his skin was icy. She picked him up and held him tightly. After several anxious minutes, she saw his color and warmth return.

Spring also returned at last. Soon after Marina and Yo-Yo rejoined Hiao-Tsiun and Yeou-Cheng in the one-room apartment, the family had a stroke of luck. A two-room apartment in the same building opened up and the Mas moved into it. Marina and the children slept in one room. Hiao-Tsiun used the other as his studio and squeezed a sleeping cot for himself into it.

Yeou-Cheng's music teacher had jokingly said that Yo-Yo could sleep on top of the piano after he was born. Of course that never happened. But a Ma "baby" did "sleep" there. One of Hiao-Tsiun's dreams was to establish a children's orchestra. He spent a great deal of time in his room, developing musical scores that would be suitable for such a group. It didn't take long for thousands of pages of music to emerge. There was hardly any extra space in the tiny room. The top of the piano was a natural place for him to put some of the scores while he worked on getting his "baby" born.

Leading a children's orchestra wasn't Hiao-Tsiun's only dream. He had a theory that good musicians were the product of three generations. The first generation provided enough money for the second generation to become well-educated. Members of the third generation, taking advantage of the education their parents provided, would become the actual musicians. Having obtained his doctorate degree in music, Hiao-Tsiun, as the "middle man," the second generation, definitely fit the pattern. There was no doubt about the high level of his learning. The true test of the theory would come with the third generation: with Yo-Yo.

Even as a toddler, Yo-Yo gave indications that he would fit into this pattern. Yeou-Cheng, a diligent and gifted student, gave her first public performance when she was about seven and a half. When it was over, she asked little Yo-Yo—who was barely three—how she had done.

He assured her that she had indeed played very well. But after a brief hesitation, he added that she had been slightly off key.

How much? she wanted to know.

As his mother explained, "He quickly replied in French, '*Une petite virgule*'—just a little comma. The amazing thing about it all was that Yo-Yo was not familiar with a single note of that musical selection!"[12]

Even earlier—by the time he turned two—he had demonstrated to his mother that he had perfect pitch. Also known as absolute pitch, perfect pitch means that someone can instantly identify a musical note without hearing any other notes.

In other words, Yo-Yo Ma was already demonstrating some of the classic indications that he was a child prodigy. According to writer Alyssa Quart, a likely prodigy herself who wrote her first novel when she was just seven, a prodigy is "a child with a skill set or an ability that is incredibly accomplished, far beyond their years."[13]

There is general agreement that heredity is one of the components of being a child prodigy. The environment that surrounds a prodigy also is a factor. Both of these elements seem to have been present for Yo-Yo. His parents were obviously gifted musically. And almost from the time of his birth, Yo-Yo was immersed in music. Classical music albums were one of the few luxuries that the Mas permitted themselves. If the family phonograph wasn't playing Bach, Beethoven, or Brahms, the infant was likely to hear his father or his sister as they practiced.

Being a child prodigy can be a double-edged sword. Quart noted that, "Designating children as gifted, especially extremely gifted, and cultivating that giftedness may be not only a waste of money, but positively harmful. The overcultivated can develop self-esteem problems and performance anxiety."[14]

The Mas were well aware of the pitfalls that could lie in wait for their son. Both Marina and Hiao-Tsiun had devoted their lives to music, and thus far they had relatively little financially to show for this devotion. While the writer of the Gospel of St. Matthew wasn't thinking about musicians when he wrote "Many are called, but few are chosen" (Matt. 20:16), his words summed up the dilemma of many seeking a living from their chosen field of art.

A famous musical joke makes much the same point. According to the joke, a drummer and a guitarist are standing on a street corner, trying to hail a taxi. Which one is the professional musician?

Answer: the taxi driver.

Not unreasonably, Marina wanted to be cautious about sealing little Yo-Yo's destiny early. "Let's just wait and see what life holds, how things develop," she told her husband. "We'll make music just a part of his education; we'll not try to influence him in any way to become a professional musician."[15]

But not long after Marina's suggestion, Hiao-Tsiun said, "Our child is gifted. I'm going to make a musician of him."[16] As had been the case with the issue of his son's birth a few years earlier, his was the final word on the subject.

Almost exactly two centuries earlier, another father had made the same decision. That father was Leopold Mozart, and his son, Wolfgang Amadeus Mozart, was by far the most famous child prodigy in music. While Mozart is most noted as a composer—many people regard him as the greatest classical composer of all time—he was also a very talented pianist at an early age. He gave his first public performance when he was five.

Yo-Yo Ma's life echoes Mozart's in interesting ways. He was born almost exactly two hundred years after Mozart, whose birth date was January 27, 1756. Both Yo-Yo and Mozart had a sister who was about four and a half years older and also very talented musically. Maria Anna ("Nannerl") Mozart, a gifted pianist, was born on June 30, 1751, and frequently appeared in concerts with her brother. Yeou-Cheng Ma also often performed with her brother, and she was born exactly 200 years and four weeks after Nannerl.

There is a third element known to be present in the development of prodigies—very involved parents. In the case of Mozart's children, this parental involvement came primarily from their father, Leopold, who was a skilled musician, teacher, and composer. He was tireless in promoting his talented offspring and accompanied them on concert tours that sometimes lasted for months. Leopold Mozart is a somewhat controversial figure. Some historians regard him as a shameless exploiter who used his children for financial gain and ruthlessly controlled their lives. Others maintain that he was an outstanding teacher who laid the foundations for his son's future greatness.

Like Mozart and like his own sister, Yo-Yo began playing the piano at an early age. Soon his father wanted him to add another instrument. The violin seemed the natural choice. He could use the same one that Yeou-Cheng had used in the beginning—a not-unreasonable move for the cash-strapped family.

It quickly became evident that Yo-Yo didn't like the instrument. "I don't like the sound the violin makes; I want a big instrument,"[17] he told his father. Hiao-Tsiun had been a teacher for a long time. He knew that it was pointless to try to force anyone—even his own son—to do something musically that he or she didn't want to do.

His solution was to compromise. He inserted an end pin into a viola, an instrument slightly larger than a violin. The end pin, placed at the lowest part of the viola's curved body, enabled the viola to be stood upright like a tiny cello. That experiment went nowhere. Even with the added length provided by the end pin, the viola wasn't big enough to satisfy Yo-Yo.

The problem moved a step closer to resolution when Hiao-Tsiun took Yo-Yo and Yeou-Cheng to hear a New Orleans jazz band. Yo-Yo was mesmerized by the musician playing the double bass. He told his father that the double bass was the instrument he wanted to play.

Immediately he created a problem. The double bass is the largest instrument in the string section of an orchestra. Even full-grown musicians can't sit but have to stand alongside their instrument just to play it. Clearly it was not suitable for a three-year-old. The stalemate between father and little son continued.

Yo-Yo kept asking his father when he would get his "big instrument." His father waited several months, hoping that, as often happens with children, his young son would forget about wanting a "big instrument" and move on to other interests. Not Yo-Yo. He continued badgering his father.

Finally Hiao-Tsiun went to Etienne Vatelot, a notable Parisian luthier (a person who makes or repairs stringed instruments) for advice.

"Let him have it," Vatelot said. "I know Yo-Yo. He will give you no peace until he holds a 'big instrument' in his hands. I have a feeling it is a sign that something good will come out of it."[18]

As events would demonstrate, of course, Vatelot quite understated the outcome. "Something truly remarkable," not just "something good," would have been a more accurate description of what the future held in store for Yo-Yo and the entire musical world.

NOTES

1. Robert Hatch and William Hatch, *The Hero Project* (New York: McGraw Hill, 2006), p. 87.

2. David Blum, *Quintet: Five Journeys Toward Musical Fulfillment* (Ithaca, N.Y.: Cornell University Press, 1999), p. 7.

3. Marina Ma, as told to John A. Rallo, *My Son, Yo-Yo* (Hong Kong: The Chinese University Press, 1995), p. 6.

4. Edith Eisler, "Yo-Yo Ma: Music from the Soul," *Strings* (May/June 1992): 48.

5. Joshua Kosman, "35 Who Made a Difference: Yo-Yo Ma," *Smithsonian* (November 2005), http://www.smithsonianmagazine.com/issues/2005/November/ma.htm.

6. Kassia Sing, personal interview with the author, May 23, 2007.

7. Ibid.

8. Ibid.

9. Janet Tassel, "Yo-Yo Ma's Journeys," *Harvard Magazine* (March–April 2000): http://harvardmagazine.com/2000/03/yo-yo-mas-journeys.html.

10. Ibid.

11. Evan Eisenberg, "Music: Through College and Life, In Harmony," *New York Times*, July 15, 2001.

12. Ma, *My Son, Yo-Yo*, p. 28.

13. Andrea Sachs, "The Downside of Being a Child Prodigy," *Time* magazine, September 6, 2006, http://www.time.com/time/arts/article/0,8599,1532087,00.html.

14. Ibid.

15. Ma, *My Son, Yo-Yo*, p. 24.

16. Ibid., p. 27.

17. Ibid., p. 29.

18. Ibid., p. 31.

Chapter 3

YO-YO GETS A "BIG LITTLE VIOLA"

Vatelot suggested a cello, or violoncello, as it is more formally known. The violoncello is smaller than a double bass, but is considerably larger than a violin or viola. Cello players sit with the instrument between their legs and use a bow to produce musical sounds. On occasion, when the music they are playing calls for it, they will pluck the strings with their fingers.

The violoncello's origins can be dated back several centuries. The roots of its name go back much further, to the Roman era and a minor Roman goddess. Named Vitula, she presided over celebrations of joy, in particular the joy following a military victory. Of course, music was an integral part of these celebrations, and her name eventually took several paths toward becoming the modern-day names of several musical instruments. One path led to England, where *Vitula* became *fithula* and *fidula*, which in turn led to the modern word "fiddle." Another path led to continental Europe, where *Vitula* became *vyell* during the medieval period.

At this point, the situation becomes somewhat complicated because the names of numerous instruments were derived from the single word *vyell*. Furthermore, though the modern forms of the names of many stringed instruments are derived from Italian, it appears that their origins might have actually been Spanish. The Spanish *vihuela* became *viola* as it traveled to Italy, probably in the sixteenth century. In 1658, Vincenzo Galilei, the father of Galileo, wrote, "In Spain one finds the first music ever written for violas, but the most ancient instruments are now found in Bologna, Brescia, Padua, and Florence."[1] Both Spain and Italy, then, can lay claim to origins of modern-day musical instruments, names, and compositions.

The musical instruments scenario becomes even more complex because at times different instruments had the same name. For example, the word *viola* and its variations became applied to all stringed instruments played with a bow.

One variation was the viola da gamba, or "viola of the legs." (The somewhat politically incorrect term "gams," referring to legs, comes from the same root.) The name referred to the fact that musicians had to hold the instrument between their legs to draw the bow across its strings. It was very similar in shape to the cello. Audiences loved its tone. For many years, the viola da gamba and its offshoots dominated the musical world. The primary difference between the viola da gamba and the violoncello—which would eventually cause the viola da gamba's decline in popularity—was that its pleasant tone was relatively weak.

Another variation of the viola was the violino, or "little viola," which morphed into the violin. A third variation was the violone, or "big viola." It had the same basic shape as the violin and viola, but was considerably larger than either—too large, in fact, to be of practical use.

By the middle of the seventeenth century, still another instrument had emerged: larger than the violin, smaller than the violone, it was known as the violoncello. Its name, broken down into its constituent roots, means "big little viola" (just as the name "Monticello," which Thomas Jefferson gave to his estate in Virginia, means "little mountain"). Because "violoncello" was a mouthful, the name was shortened to 'cello. Eventually the apostrophe was abandoned and the instrument's name became simply cello. (In a similar manner, the pianoforte—which means "soft loud"—became simply piano.)

Over time, the violin, viola, and cello displaced the viola da gamba. The former group proved to have greater capacity for expression. They also had a more powerful sound, which became a factor as music moved out of drawing rooms and into larger performance venues.

This transition wasn't always a smooth process. Many aristocrats—and the men who composed for them—were opposed to the usurpers. One composer sniffed that the violin was suitable only for "dances and processions."[2] Another asserted that the cello was "a wretched, despised poor devil, who instead of starving to death as could well be expected, now even boasts of replacing the bass viola da gamba."[3] But replace was exactly what the cello did, though the viola da gamba still has its adherents today.

At first, though, the cello was used primarily as part of the basso continuo, the instrumental accompaniment to the melodic line during the Baroque era. It began to emerge as an instrument in its own right near the end of the seventeenth century. At that time composers such as Alessandro and Domenico Scarletti, Benedetto Marcello, and above all the "Red Priest," Antonio Vivaldi (who wrote 27 cello concertos, many of which Yo-Yo would later record), recognized its power and ability to communicate profound emotion.

It was left to Johann Sebastian Bach to break new musical ground—as he did in so many other areas—with his six suites for solo cello. Bach was especially renowned as an organist, but he was also adept as a string player, particularly on the violin and viola. Scholars note that each one of the six cello suites is technically more difficult than its predecessor, and speculate that he wrote them to explore the cello's tonal potential for future compositions.

The instrument received another boost in popularity with the advent of Luigi Boccherini, who was regarded as the first truly great cello virtuoso, in the latter part of the eighteenth century. Boccherini took advantage of his extensive musical knowledge and his audience drawing power to write 10 cello concertos and 30 sonatas for cello. Franz Josef Haydn followed closely on his heels, and Haydn's two cello concertos are among the most highly regarded compositions in the entire literature for the cello.

The cello truly came into its own during the Romantic era (about 1815–1910) as composers began to take advantage of the instrument's rich tones. According to music historian Frederick L. Kirshnit, Robert Schumann's Cello Concerto, written in 1850, was "a Romantic outpouring of intense feeling . . . the cello actually becomes a singer of beautiful, lyrical music (this is the moment in music history where the cello, for the first time, realizes its true potential)."[4]

It was at about this time, around the middle of the nineteenth century, that cellists began outfitting their instruments with end pins. End pins are about a foot in length; they allow the musicians to rest their cellos on the ground, thereby removing the necessity of having strong leg muscles for gripping the cello in place while it is being played. Some people believe that the endpin also increases the resonance of the cello's sound, especially when playing on stages with wooden floors, whose vibration supplements that of the cello.

Robert Schumann was an influence on a slightly later composer, Johannes Brahms, who wrote several major compositions for the cello, including the Double Concerto—more formally, the Concerto for Violin, Cello, and Orchestra, written in 1887. Brahms in turn exerted an influence on Antonin Dvořák, who, in 1895, wrote Concerto for Cello in B Minor, which is perhaps the most popular cello concerto. In writing the piece, Dvořák was influenced by the recent death of his first great love, Josefina Kaunitzova (Dvořák later married her sister Anna). Says historian Kirshnit, "[T]he finale contains one of the great endings in concert music. The solo part becomes softer and softer, '. . . like a sigh . . .' Dvořák wrote to his publisher, before the orchestra concludes the piece at a loud volume."[5]

The last significant composition during the nineteenth century was Richard Strauss's tone poem *Don Quixote*, composed in 1897. Strauss chose the cello to portray Don Quixote in a musical exploration of important scenes inspired by the novel by Miguel de Cervantes.

In addition to cello concertos, frequently the centerpieces of live concerts, composers also wrote significant amounts of chamber music (music for a small group of instruments) featuring the cello. Furthermore, many composers included significant solo passages for the cello in their compositions written specifically for an entire orchestra. The trend continued into the twentieth century. Many composers had written and were still writing concertos and other works for the cello by the time of Yo-Yo's birth.

Because a full-sized cello would dwarf Yo-Yo, Vatelot made a smaller version of the instrument. Yo-Yo was delighted. It was only much later that he confided the real reason why he wanted a "big instrument" to his mother. He was in awe of his sister's playing and didn't feel that he could match her accomplishments.

Having acceded to his son's request in this regard, Hiao-Tsiun was determined that Yo-Yo would follow his other precepts. Hiao-Tsiun was a very disciplined man. He insisted that his students establish the discipline of constant practice. Yet he also realized that children couldn't put in the long hours of practice that would be routine for an adult. As a result, he had developed a different approach to teaching children to play music. It was natural for him to want to use his children as "guinea pigs" to test his theories.

One of his methods was breaking up practice sessions into shorter intervals. Another was to implement his belief in the absolute necessity of memorization. He gave his son an assignment: every day Yo-Yo would learn to play two measures of one of Bach's suites for solo cello. A measure is the basic building block of a musical score. Each measure is indicated by a vertical line in the musical staff called a barline. Frequently a measure consists of one accented beat followed by one or more unaccented beats. Yo-Yo's assignment would contain a total of at least four beats.

Hiao-Tsiun believed in the power of repetition. "I had to play right," Yo-Yo recalled. "If I made a mistake, then I would have to play the passage right three consecutive times."[6]

In the beginning this process was easy. The young musician gained confidence by mastering the first few measures and being able to quickly recall and play them. This confidence helped him as he moved deeper into the composition his father had assigned.

Yo-Yo would need all the confidence he could get. The Bach suites are regarded as especially difficult to play, even for accomplished cellists with years or even decades of experience. Giving difficult works such as these to his son was somewhat equivalent to throwing a nonswimmer into the deep end of a pool. On the other hand, learning the music slowly but surely was not unlike giving him water wings, allowing the boy to gain confidence before becoming fully immersed.

The method seems to have worked very well. Within a year, Yo-Yo had learned to play three of the suites. But Hiao-Tsiun knew his own limitations. He wasn't a cellist. He realized that although he had gotten Yo-Yo off to a solid start, the boy needed formal lessons from an experienced cello teacher. Hiao-Tsiun had already arranged for the well-known violinist Arthur Grumiaux to work with his daughter. He chose Michelle Lepinte to be Yo-Yo's teacher.

Lepinte was shocked to find that Yo-Yo had already learned to play the Bach suites, regarding them as difficult even for much older students. She was equally shocked and astonished when the youngster played the pieces flawlessly for her. It was evident that he was far above her other students in terms of talent and skill level, and able to assimilate what she had to offer at a much faster pace.

Many years later, Yo-Yo still had fond memories of Lepinte. "She was a wonderful French lady," he recalled. "The reason I loved my first cello teacher was that she was so nice; I could never do anything wrong. I think she made me love the cello . . . and I liked her perfume also."[7]

Yo-Yo flourished under Lepinte's tutelage. One result was the emergence of still another similarity between Yo-Yo and Mozart. Like Mozart, Yo-Yo gave his first public performance when he was five, as part of a 1961 group recital at the Institute of Art and Archeology at the University of Paris.

The recital demonstrated two things. One was the outstanding quality of his performance. The other was that even at such a young age, he understood some fundamental principles of showmanship. He had already exhibited his grasp of this quality at the time he commented on the early performance by his sister, when he had noted that she was slightly off: not only had he been attentive to her playing, but he had also found time to count the house to see how many patrons were in attendance.

Because Hiao-Tsiun didn't want to tax his son's energy, he only planned on having Yo-Yo play one section of a Bach suite at the concert. However, Yo-Yo wanted to play the entire piece. Though his father shook his head, the youngster came up with a true showman's solution. He told his parents to applaud loudly when he finished the selection. The audience would be inspired to do the same thing. That way it would seem like they all wanted him to keep playing. He was right. He received applause after each section and was permitted to play the entire suite.

Soon afterward, Hiao-Tsiun received a letter from his brother Hiao-Jone, who lived in Rochester, New York. This letter would completely transform the Mas' life.

Hiao-Jone had also left China, and he and his family had lived in the United States for a number of years. Now, Hiao-Jone told his brother, he wanted to go back to China. Hiao-Tsiun was horrified. Though the Communists had seized control of China in 1949, conditions in the country remained chaotic. The Chinese economy was still in tatters, and widespread famine had claimed the lives of many people. In addition, Chinese leader Mao Zedong faced opposition from within the ruling Communist Party, further threatening the stability of the government. On top of everything else, official opposition to authors and other artists who didn't toe the party line had begun. This opposition would culminate in the Cultural Revolution in 1966, and result in the deaths of many dissidents.

In short, Hiao-Tsiun believed that it would be the height of folly for his brother to return.

He sent him a letter that detailed the reasons why Hiao-Jone should remain where he was, at least until China became more peaceful. The letter did not dissuade Hiao-Jone. Then Hiao-Tsiun made a long-distance phone call to his brother, which at that time was a complicated and expensive undertaking. The call had no more effect than the letter. Hiao-Jone was still determined to return to China.

To Hiao-Tsiun, that left just one alternative. He would fly to the United States and try to talk Hiao-Jone out of his decision. Hiao-Tsiun's family would accompany him. At that time, flying across the Atlantic Ocean was still an adventure. It was not something to be undertaken lightly.

The trip was successful. Hiao-Tsiun talked his brother into staying in the United States. With the problem resolved, the two families spent a month with each other. During that time Hiao-Tsiun made arrangements for Yo-Yo to give his first American performance. Held at Nazareth College in Rochester, the program began with Yo-Yo and Yeou-Cheng appearing on stage together. Then Yo-Yo performed one of the Bach suites by himself.

Shortly after that concert, the family took the opportunity of being in America to do some more visiting. They traveled across the country to Berkeley, California, to visit Marina's sister.

After they returned to New York, they spent a few days in Manhattan. Hiao-Tsiun was enthralled by the bustle and energy of the city, which he was seeing for the first time. He stood reverently in front of Carnegie Hall, the city's most famous concert venue, and dreamed of seeing his son's name on the marquee. The sight inspired him to stage a recital that featured his talented children. But he wasn't familiar enough with New York to select an appropriate venue. One of Hiao-Jone's friends could help: he knew of a nearby Catholic church that would offer its auditorium for free.

Besides showing off his accomplished young family, Hiao-Tsiun had a more practical reason for putting on the concert. As Yeou-Cheng explained, "We had spent our life's savings to come to America, and in order to go back to Paris, we had to give a few concerts."[8]

No matter the reason, the performance would turn out to be completely life-changing. One of the people in the audience would make Hiao-Tsiun an offer he couldn't refuse.

NOTES

1. Carlos Prieto, *The Adventures of a Cello*, translated by Elena C. Murray (Austin, Tex.: Texas University Press, 2006), p. 5.

2. Ibid., p. 7.

3. Ibid.

4. Frederick L. Kirshnit, "Instruments of Mass Seduction—Part I: The Cello," ConcertoNet.com—the Classical Music Network, http://www.concertonet.com/scripts/edito.php?ID_edito=60.

5. Ibid.

6. "Yo-Yo's Way with the Strings," *Time*, January 19, 1981, http://www.time.com/time/printout/0,8816,924666,00.html.

7. "From the Top: Radio and Television: Hall of Fame—Yo-Yo Ma," http://www.fromthetop.org/Programs/HallOfFame.cfm?pid=1858.

8. Edith Eisler, "The Music Doctor: Yeou-Cheng Ma's Double Career," *Strings*, March–April (1995): 57.

Chapter 4

A NEW LIFE IN NEW YORK

Isalina Davidson was the founder and director of the Trent School, a small private school in Manhattan. She had long envisioned establishing a children's orchestra in her school, especially since she had two sons who were stringed instrument players. But she hadn't been able to find anyone to lead it. As she listened to the exquisite sounds that Yo-Yo and Yeou-Cheng coaxed from their respective instruments, she realized that the children's father was just the person she was looking for.

As soon as the concert was over, she hurried up to Hiao-Tsiun and offered him a job. For Hiao-Tsiun, the offer must have seemed like a dream come true. All the long hours he had spent developing the scores for a children's orchestra suddenly looked as though they might actually come to fruition. The Children's Orchestra Society came into being soon afterward. It is still in existence.

Hiao-Tsiun's new job as orchestra master held other attractions as well. One was its proximity to artistic opportunities in addition to the children's orchestra. For many years, the United States had languished in the shadow of Europe as a venue for the arts. After World War II, the United States became an international superpower politically. It was also attaining superpower stature in the arts. New York City, with its wealth of museums and theaters plus performing arts organizations such as the Metropolitan Opera and the New York Philharmonic Orchestra, was front and center in America's burgeoning cultural importance. What better place could there be for Yo-Yo to develop his talent and put it on display?

Also, living in New York would get the Mas out of their limited quarters in Paris. As the children continued to grow, that already tiny space seemed to contract even further.

There would be still another change. Yo-Yo and Yeou-Cheng would begin attending school. While the Ma family was living in Paris, their father had been their teacher in every aspect of his children's education, not just in music. By all reports, he had a special gift for imparting knowledge. A widespread story that he taught a dog to sing Chopin's "Minute Waltz" is likely to have been an exaggeration, but Yeou-Cheng affirmed that, "He could teach anybody anything, whether or not he could do it himself. He taught me Bible stories even though he was an atheist, and touch-typing without being able to touch-type."[1]

First the Mas had to return to Paris to get ready for their permanent move. They bought English language records and began a crash course in what would become their third language, after Chinese and French. In the midst of their preparations, Yo-Yo became involved in what could have been a very serious accident.

It occurred while he was trying to open a stuck window. The glass shattered as he pushed ever harder and shards sliced deeply into his wrist. His mother applied a tourniquet to try to stop the copious bleeding, then appealed to a taxi driver neighbor to take them to the hospital. The man said he couldn't because company rules wouldn't allow him to drive out of a certain zone.

Fortunately, another neighbor happened to be home, heard the commotion, and drove them to the hospital. A doctor quickly treated Yo-Yo. He said that Marina had brought the little boy to him just in time. If she had delayed much longer, he explained, Yo-Yo could have suffered permanent damage to his wrist. Such damage almost certainly would have ended his cello career before it had a chance to get started.

The family completed their preparations and left Paris for good. When they arrived in New York, one of their first priorities was finding a teacher for Yo-Yo. Hiao-Tsiun chose Janos Scholz. Born in Hungary, Scholz became a highly regarded cellist in early 1930s Europe. Following Adolf Hitler's rise to power in Germany in 1933, conditions in Europe became so unsettled that Scholz fled to the United States. He became active in the New York music scene as a soloist, as a member of several performing groups, and as a teacher.

Not long after Yo-Yo began his lessons with Scholz, the family met noted violinist Alexander Schneider, a member of the highly regarded Budapest Quartet. Schneider politely agreed to hear Yo-Yo play. Thoroughly impressed by what he heard, he asked, "Has Pablo heard him play?"[2]

"Pablo" was Spanish-born Pablo Casals, almost certainly the greatest cellist in the world in the first half of the twentieth century—and in the opinion of many people, the greatest cellist of all time. Casals was born in late 1876, barely six months after Custer's Last Stand, and would live long enough to watch the first humans land on the moon. His audiences included Queen Victoria of England and U.S. President John F. Kennedy. He learned to play the violin, the piano, and the flute by the age of four. Seven years later, a chamber music trio—a pianist, a violinist, and a cellist—gave a concert that Casals attended with his father. It was the first time he had heard the cello and—very similar to what had happened with Yo-Yo—it was love at first sight.

"From the moment I heard the first notes I was overwhelmed," he recalled. "There was something so tender, beautiful, and human—yes, so very human—about the sound. I had never heard such a beautiful sound before. A radiance filled me. When the first composition was ended, I told my father, 'Father, that is the most wonderful instrument I have ever heard.' . . . From that time, more than eighty years ago, I was wedded to the instrument. It would be my companion and friend for the rest of my life."[3]

Within a few years Casals became internationally celebrated. Writing in 1913, music critic W. J. Turner said, "His playing . . . is one of those rare things that may only come once in a lifetime and even not in one person's life, it may be centuries before there is anyone like that again. He is a funny little fellow only about 30 and plays with his eyes shut practically the whole time, every note every pause and tone colour is reflected in his face and to hear him again, to draw the bow across is a revelation."[4]

Casals' stature only increased during the succeeding decades, partly on the basis of his musical accomplishments, partly because of his principled stands on political and social issues. During the Spanish Civil War, he was firmly and very publicly on the Republican side. One of Nationalist leader Francisco Franco's most prominent aides vowed to cut off Casals' arms at the elbows if he were captured. Undeterred, Casals continued his efforts on behalf of the Republicans. When it appeared inevitable that Franco's forces would win the war and establish a fascist government, Casals reluctantly left his country and vowed never to return until Franco was overthrown. From then on, he always closed his concerts with "The Song of the Birds," a folk song from his native region of Catalonia.

Advancing age hardly seemed to slow him down. He developed into an important conductor and composer. Like Yo-Yo, he was recognized by the United Nations. In 1971, he received the organization's Medal of Peace for his work in opposing war and advancing the cause of peace. In honor of the occasion, he composed "Hymn of the United Nations." He was 95 at the time.

In view of Casals' monumental stature in the music world, it isn't surprising that in 1962 Hiao-Tsiun leaped at the chance for him to listen to Yo-Yo. Alexander Schneider was a good friend of Casals and arranged a meeting. Soon afterward Yo-Yo and his family walked into the great man's apartment. Though it was the first time that the two had actually met, Casals had unknowingly already exercised a great deal of influence on Yo-Yo.

Yo-Yo began his cello career by learning the Bach suites. Nearly half a century earlier, Casals had played the primary role in the suites' becoming a vital part, perhaps even the centerpiece, of the commonly accepted cello repertoire. A year or two after taking up the cello, Casals had been hired to play in a café. He proved to be such a popular attraction that many patrons returned on a regular basis to hear him play. To satisfy them, he continually needed new music so they wouldn't become bored by hearing him play the same compositions over and over again.

Accompanied by his father one day, he went into a music shop and began rummaging among the cello scores to see if he could find something that he hadn't already played. Nearly 80 years later, he easily recalled his excitement at what came next: "Suddenly I came upon a sheaf of pages, crumbled and discolored with age. They were unaccompanied suites by Johann Sebastian Bach—for the cello only! . . . I had never heard of the existence of the suites; nobody—not even my teachers—had ever mentioned them to me. . . . I hurried home, clutching the suites as if they were the crown jewels, and once in my room I pored over them. I read and reread them. I was thirteen at the time, but for the following eighty years the wonder of my discovery has continued to grow on me."[5]

It has grown on others as well. Virtually every notable twentieth-century cellist has played the suites. One of the most notable—and moving—performances came in 1989. That year, the famous Russian cellist Mstislav Rostropovich, like Casals an outspoken opponent of totalitarianism, dropped everything to fly to Berlin when he saw the infamous Berlin Wall being torn down. He took a taxi to the site, borrowed a chair, sat down, and began to play.

"Within 10 minutes, there was a little crowd, and a television crew came passing by," he said. "I played the most joyous Bach Suites for solo cello in order to celebrate the event. But I could not forget all those who had lost their lives on this wall in trying to cross over it. Hence, I played the *Sarabande* of Bach's 2nd Suite in their memory, and I noticed a young man crying."[6]

A century earlier, such a scene would have been regarded as an impossibility. Prior to Casals' discovery, Bach's religious choral compositions were virtually his only works regarded as suitable for public performance. His orchestral compositions were regarded as stiff, academic music. This perception stunned Casals. "How could anyone think of them as being cold, when a whole radiance of space and poetry pours forth from them?" he said. "They are the very essence of Bach, and Bach is the very essence of music."[7]

In spite of his passion for the suites, it took Casals more than 13 years to work up enough courage to play them in public. When he did, he changed the face of the musical landscape. As a result, Casals is forever identified with the Bach suites. While Yo-Yo Ma's career has become even more diverse than Casals', as a cellist he too is primarily defined by the same music.

The suites are a unique blend of invention and tradition. Bach broke new musical ground in terms of the increasing complexity he employed in composing his suites, yet he used an existing form for his model, known as the *suite de danses*. This musical form had begun its development well over a century before Bach's birth year, 1685. Serendipitously, the *suite de danses* presaged Yo-Yo's own interest in drawing from disparate sources, for it consisted of four stylized dances from different countries: the allemande (Germany), courante (France), sarabande (Spain), and gigue (England). The allemande and sarabande were relatively slow and stately, while the courante and gigue provided contrast with their more brisk tempos. Despite having its origins in social dancing, however, the *suite de danses* was conceived as strictly an orchestral composition. No one envisioned it as actual dance music. The only exercise for its audiences would be applause.

Some composers—including Bach—added a prelude, and also inserted what were known as galanteries (brief dances of French origin, often based on folk dances) between the sarabande and gigue. In Bach's suites these dance pieces were the minuet (Suite Nos. 1 and 2), bourrée (Suite Nos. 3 and 4), and gavotte (Suite Nos. 5 and 6).[8]

Under Bach's hand, the suites increase in complexity as they progress. Thus the first is the easiest to play (at least in relative terms), while the sixth is the most difficult. All six challenge the most skillful of musicians.

Their complexity is not the only difficulty the suites present. Their very substance is in question. No one knows definitively what Bach actually wrote. In view of the reverence in which Bach is held today by musicians—classical and nonclassical alike—it can be jolting to realize that in the years following his death he was held in relatively low regard. There seemed little reason back then to preserve his works, and his own handwritten versions of many of his compositions simply disappeared. No original manuscripts of any of the suites are known to have been found, and no single definitive edition is in existence. There is one manuscript that his wife Anna Magdalena wrote down, and two more manuscripts penned by his students were discovered in 1960—but that's just the tip of the iceberg. Currently more than 80 different editions are extant. Scholars have endlessly debated which version is "correct."

When Yo-Yo walked into Casals' apartment for his appointment in 1962, his youth probably worked in his favor. A cellist older than Yo-Yo might well have become flustered at the thought of playing before such a legendary musician. For Yo-Yo, it must have seemed like just another opportunity to perform. He was too young to fully appreciate what a unique opportunity he had been given. He simply played. And played well.

"When the audition was over, Casals picked up Yo-Yo and sat him on his lap," Marina Ma recalled. "'Would you like to play some more?' he asked routinely, thinking that the boy would be tired after his performance.

"He should have known better. For Yo-Yo, the playing had just begun.

"'Yes, yes,' he answered beaming with such genuine excitement that the maestro just leaned back in his chair and listened as Yo-Yo's bow 'sang.'"[9]

Yo-Yo had a somewhat different memory of the encounter. "I don't remember what he said about my cello playing,"[10] he recalled. He did remember what Casals told his parents: "What are you doing with this child? You must let him go and play on the street."[11]

For Hiao-Tsiun, such words would have been anathema. His plans for his son didn't include playing on the street. In his opinion, it was not only a waste of time, it was potentially dangerous. Something bad could easily happen. To make sure that that it didn't, Hiao-Tsiun laid out a rigid daily structure for his children that governed virtually every aspect of their lives.

Years later, Yo-Yo reflected on the reasons for this rigidity. "The demand for perfection, all that pressure, came from the wars," he said. "My parents had anguished lives. They saw antiques chopped up for fuel, all sorts of violence, and that left them with the sense that all that lasts are skills."[12]

This regimen might have worked indefinitely in China or even in Paris. The United States was a very different story. In later life, Yo-Yo recalled the issue. "As soon as we moved to America I had to deal with two contradictory worlds. At home, I was to submerge my identity. You can't talk back to your parents. At school, I was expected to answer back, to reveal my individuality."[13]

The conflict between the two worlds would not fully emerge for several more years. In the meantime, Casals was so impressed with what he heard from Yo-Yo that he immediately undercut his own advice to send the boy to play out on the streets. Casals had been invited to perform on November 29 in a benefit concert to help construct a performing arts venue in Washington, D.C. The program was to be conducted by Leonard Bernstein and was entitled "The American Pageant of the Arts." It would be televised on a pay-per-view basis in dozens of cities across the United States. Casals contacted Bernstein and encouraged him to add Yo-Yo and his sister to the already star-studded roster of performers.

On November 19, 1962, the New York Times reported that "the show will have a cast of 100, including President and Mrs. Kennedy, Dwight D. Eisenhower, Leonard Bernstein (as master of ceremonies), Pablo Casals, Marian Anderson, Van Cliburn, Robert Frost, Fredric March, Benny Goodman, Bob Newhart and a 7-year-old Chinese cellist named Yo-yo Ma, who was brought to the program's attention by Casals."[14]

The article was noteworthy in two respects. First, it included Yo-Yo's name in the same sentence as those of two U.S. presidents and eight world-famous performers and writers. Second, Yo-Yo had been identified in a major newspaper for the first time. It would hardly be the last. In the years since then, the New York Times alone has written about him more than 1,000 times.

It was a heady experience for the seven-year-old. Not only was this to be his first time on live television, he would also be just a few feet away from President John F. Kennedy. Not surprisingly, he was nervous before the performance. But his nervousness had little to do with the conditions under which he would be performing. He was still playing an undersized cello, and was afraid that the sound wouldn't carry throughout the auditorium. His father assured him that there was nothing to worry about. There would be nearby loudspeakers and everyone would be able to hear him just fine. With that concern out of the way, Yo-Yo relaxed and played to the full extent of his abilities. It may have helped that he wasn't performing alone. Yeou-Cheng accompanied him on the piano. When they were finished, they took a curtain call with Leonard Bernstein to thunderous applause.

The following day, a leading Washington, D.C., newspaper, The Evening Star, echoed the response of the audience: "Child prodigy Yo-Yo Ma, seven-year old cellist, who is accompanied on the piano by his 11-year-old sister, thrills the multitude at the Armory gathered to hear the special benefit show to promote the building of a National Cultural Center here."[15]

The concert was successful, raising more than $1 million to help with the cost of building the new structure. Tragically, President Kennedy was assassinated slightly less than a year after the concert. The structure was named the John F. Kennedy Center for the Performing Arts in his honor. In the upcoming years, Yo-Yo would make frequent appearances at the venue he had helped build.

The Ma family returned home in triumph. Yo-Yo and his sister continued their music lessons and worked hard in their classes at the Trent School, while Hiao-Tsiun continued to develop his children's orchestra.

It wouldn't be too long before the family—and Yo-Yo in particular—would undergo some major changes.

NOTES

1. Edith Eisler, "The Music Doctor: Yeou-Cheng Ma's Double Career," *Strings* (March/April 1995), pp. 56–57.

2. Marina Ma, as told to John A. Rallo, *My Son, Yo-Yo* (Hong Kong: The Chinese University Press, 1995), p. 81.

3. Pablo Casals, *Joys and Sorrows: His Own Story as Told to Albert E. Kahn* (New York: Simon and Schuster, 1970), pp. 35–36.

4. "Pablo Casals," http://en.wikiquote.org/wiki/Pablo_Casals.

5. Casals, *Joys and Sorrows*, p. 46.

6. "Six French Interviews with Mstislav Rostropovich, November 2005 to November 2006," translated by David Abrams, http://www.cello.org/Newsletter/Articles/rostrofrench/rostrofrench.htm

7. Casals, *Joys and Sorrows*, p. 47.

8. *The Water Music* by Bach's exact contemporary George Fridrich Handel is probably the most famous composition to employ the suite form. It actually consists of three separate suites, and departs from the traditional form that Bach used by substituting several different dances, primarily the minuet, bourrée, and hornpipe. According to reports, King George I, for whom it was composed, liked it so much that he requested two encores of the entire piece when it premiered on July 17, 1717.

Handel's much shorter *Music for the Royal Fireworks*—which consists of a single suite—represented the last hurrah of the *suite de danses* when it premiered in 1749. By that time the rise of classical forms had rendered the traditional suite obsolete as the symphony and concerto had become the dominant musical forms.

The suite made a comeback about a century later, though by then it had changed to encompass either selections from a longer work (such as Tchaikovsky's

Nutcracker Suite) or a series of short compositions linked by a common theme (such as Edvard Grieg's *Peer Gynt Suites* or *The Planets* by Gustav Holst).

9. Ma, *My Son, Yo-Yo*, pp. 81–82.

10. David Blum, *Quintet: Five Journeys Toward Musical Fulfillment* (Ithaca, NY: Cornell University Press, 1999), pp. 10–11.

11. "Yo-Yo's Way with the Strings," *Time*, January 19, 1981, http://www.time.com/time/printout/0,8816,924666,00.html.

12. Leslie Rubinstein, "Oriental Musicians Come of Age," *New York Times*, November 23, 1980.

13. Blum, *Quintet*, p. 10.

14. Arthur Gelb, "Spectacle on Closed-Circuit TV to Herald Cultural Center Drive," *New York Times*, November 19, 1962.

15. Ma, *My Son, Yo-Yo*, p. 151.

Chapter 5

HIGH SCHOOL AND
HIGH ANXIETY

Yo-Yo did not remain with the Trent School for long. In 1964 he began attending another school, the École Française. Some of the classes were conducted in French, which didn't pose any problem for Yo-Yo since he had been raised speaking French during the first six years of his life.

His classmates included the children of some of New York City's most famous singers, actors, and other performing artists. Therefore when the school decided to hold a fundraiser that December featuring performances by many of these notable parents, it was considerably more prestigious than a similar event at other schools. It wasn't even held in the school auditorium. Instead, École Française rented Carnegie Hall. Less than three years after Hiao-Tsiun had stood in front of the same building and imagined his son performing there, his dream was about to come true.

The stature of the performers—violinist Isaac Stern, actress Diahann Carroll, ballet dancer Maria Tallchief, and numerous others—was so impressive that the *New York Times* sent music critic Robert Sherman to review the concert. His review began, "Parents' night at P.S. 9 was never like this. But then the children at l'Ecole Francaise have rather special parents. A number of the more celebrated mothers and fathers met in joyful conclave yesterday evening at Carnegie Hall, putting on a benefit concert for the school's growth and scholarship funds."[1]

The "celebrated mothers and fathers" weren't the only ones who performed. So did Hiao-Tsiun's Children's Orchestra, and also Hiao-Tsiun's own children, Yeou-Cheng and Yo-Yo. Sherman became perhaps the first major critic to sing the praises of Yo-Yo. "Yo-Yo Ma, the conductor's nine-year-old son, a cellist, then joined his twelve-year-old [sic] sister Yeou-

Cheng to play Sammartini's G Major Cello Sonata," he wrote. "This is no children's piece, nor did they play it like children. The performance had assurance, poise and a full measure of delicate musicality."[2]

Isaac Stern, who was himself performing that night and who was by then one of the most famous violinists in the world, certainly would have agreed with Sherman. He had first heard Yo-Yo four years earlier in Paris after Etienne Vatelot, the luthier who had put together the little boy's first cello, urged Stern to attend the 1961 group recital concert at the University of Paris. At that time Yo-Yo was only five years old, and Stern's first impression was that the cello seemed larger than the little boy who was playing it. His second impression upon hearing the same little boy at age nine was longer-lasting. He was utterly astonished at the sounds that Yo-Yo coaxed from his instrument and took an active step to further the boy's talent.

In the early 1950s, he had joined forces with pianist Eugene Istomin and cellist Leonard Rose to form the Istomin/Stern/Rose trio. After struggling for recognition for several years, their stature eventually rose to the point where they were regarded as among the finest chamber music groups in the world. Now Stern felt that Rose, his friend and colleague, should begin teaching Yo-Yo. Hiao-Tsiun agreed.

Rose was an illustrious figure in the music world. He was born in 1918 in Washington, D.C. At the age of eight he began taking piano lessons and added the cello two years later. He became a member of the NBC Symphony Orchestra when he was 18 and three years afterward was appointed principal cellist of the Cleveland Orchestra, one of the country's five most prestigious orchestras. In 1946 he became a professor at the Juilliard School of Music. Five years later he devoted himself to a career as a soloist and teacher. He made numerous well-received recordings and rocketed to international fame along with Istomin and Stern.

Rose's glittering accomplishments and resume came in spite of a difficult childhood. His mother was self-absorbed, frequently sad, and incapable of providing him with much warmth. His father was overly demanding and often called him stupid. Then there was the matter of being Jewish in an era when anti-Semitism was frequently evident.

"I was a chubby Jewish boy, carrying a cello and books," he recalled. "What a target I was for Jew-baiting bullies, and what a sensitive, frightened kid I was. On at least two occasions, I was surrounded by four or five larger boys, and taunted and beaten. . . . I'm afraid my psyche was very damaged by those episodes."[3] It is a tribute to Rose that he not only survived the conditions of his youth but also became thriving and productive.

Stern arranged an audition for Yo-Yo with Rose. Years later, Rose's daughter Barbara still had a vivid recollection of the event.

"When the doorbell rang, this tiny nine-year-old walked in with his little cello, with his parents trailing behind. Yo-Yo went right to the biggest chair in the living room and sat down while his parents sat on the side with the cello standing up on the floor next to them. It was the cutest scene you could imagine.

"I went to my father's studio door and gave it the special knock that indicated when a student arrived and my father came out and gestured for Yo-Yo to come in. Yo-Yo's father, who was the conductor of a youth orchestra in Brooklyn (sic), wanted to go in with his son, but my father indicated that he would rather see the child alone. Yo-Yo could care less and went in while his father stood outside the door and his mother sat on the couch.

"My mother and I were in the kitchen when we heard Yo-Yo begin to play. I turned to my mother and said, 'Oh my god. This kid is only this big,' gesturing with my hand low to the floor. My mother said, 'Really?' After the lesson, my father came in and I've never seem him so excited. He said, 'This is the best talent I've ever had!' He said, 'I can't believe it, I just can't believe it, Isaac was right.'"[4]

If Janos Scholz had any ill feelings at losing Yo-Yo as his student, he kept them carefully hidden. Years later, he said that Yo-Yo was "the most natural and eager boy you could imagine. . . . He was adored by my whole family. We went through a mountain of repertoire in two years. He learned with lightning speed. He was everything one could wish for as a student, and the last I ever took."[5]

Yo-Yo attended his lessons at the institution where Rose taught: The Juilliard School. The school had been established in 1905 as the School of Musical Art. At that time, most talented American musicians went to Europe to study and the new school's founders wanted to keep them in the United States. Its name was changed to honor Augustus Juilliard, a highly successful textile merchant, who donated most of his fortune to the school when he died in 1919. Today The Juilliard School is regarded as perhaps the best music school in the United States and among the top schools worldwide.

Working with Rose proved to be ideal. One reason was that Rose made Yo-Yo feel comfortable. "I was a pipsqueak of a kid," Yo-Yo recalled. "I was afraid to speak to Mr. Rose above a whisper. I'd try to hide behind the cello. . . . He tried to get me to overcome my timidity by constantly urging me to sing out on the instrument. I was amazed to hear phrases coming from a fifty-year-old man such as 'Sock it to me, baby!' or, to my dismay, 'Thrill me, thrill me—like my wife did this morning.'"[6]

Rose encouraged Yo-Yo by explaining that he too had been shy, but had succeeded in overcoming it. Perhaps even more important, he quickly convinced Yo-Yo that he was firmly in his corner. "He was rooting for me," Yo-Yo said. "And I think that nothing is more important than having someone, especially if you have contact with one of your heroes, to have them sort of root for you."[7]

That sense of support may have been an important stabilizer in the coming years. The reticence and shyness Rose wanted Yo-Yo to overcome stemmed in part from Yo-Yo's traditional Chinese upbringing. Ingrained habits couldn't change overnight, but little by little Yo-Yo started coming out of his shell. As he emerged from his shyness, the dichotomy he had been aware of earlier—between the two worlds of Chinese tradition and American innovation—also began to emerge. At home, his father's rule was still law and he couldn't confront him. When Yo-Yo was at school it became a different story. Starting in the fifth grade, he began cutting classes. But whatever turmoil he was experiencing about the clash of cultures didn't carry over into his cello playing; he remained a disciplined and dedicated young musician.

Because of Rose's extensive concert traveling schedule, Yo-Yo—like the majority of Rose's other students—often worked with Rose's assistant, Channing Robbins. Robbins, who worked with Rose for more than 30 years, specialized in bowing technique. He also emphasized the importance of practicing by making the piece being rehearsed more difficult than it normally would have been, in many cases by varying the way in which the student held his or her bow. That way when it was time to perform using normal bowing technique, the musician felt especially confident. A sports analogy would be for a basketball team, which has five members active on the basketball court during a game, to practice against a team of six players. If the team could succeed under those circumstances, its members would feel much more confident when they faced the usual five-member opposing team.

As Yo-Yo's musicianship blossomed, his fame began to spread. When he was 12, the family made a visit to Berkeley to visit Marina's sister. Yo-Yo was asked to appear with the San Francisco Little Symphony. There was nothing "little" about the boy's performance. As the *San Francisco Examiner*'s music critic, Arthur Bloomfield, wrote, "Would you believe me if I wrote that a bespectacled 12-year-old boy came on stage yesterday and played the cello so startlingly well that he must be counted in the same category as Starker, Rose, Varga, Piatigorsky, and Casals? Well, it's the truth."[8]

The timing of this review in Yo-Yo's life and the mention of Casals seem remarkably coincidental, for Pablo Casals was also reviewed—in his case, for the first time—at the age of 12. The unidentified critic said, "[T]he boy Paulito Casals was outstanding in the violoncello part which he developed with such masterly confidence that we have no hesitation in assuring him a brilliant future in the study of music if he continues with his present devotion and innate musical talent."[9]

Yo-Yo's devotion to his own artistry continued, but his burgeoning career did have one downside, at least by American standards of "normal." His hands were very precious and Hiao-Tsiun was no more ready to run the risk of injury to them than he had been when Casals suggested that the boy play on the street. Yo-Yo's life therefore remained rigidly regimented. He practiced for at least an hour every morning, went to school, came home, practiced some more, and then did his homework. That left little or no room for activities such as soccer, baseball, or even spending time with friends. Hiao-Tsiun's one concession to normality was to allow Yo-Yo to watch television for half an hour or an hour. Sometimes the boy would also swim at the local YMCA.

In China, this pattern could have continued indefinitely. In the United States, however, conditions were very different. Signs of Yo-Yo's dissatisfaction with his father's strict rules were beginning to become apparent. By the time of his San Francisco concert, he was already attending his third school, The Trinity School. Founded in 1709, the school is the fifth oldest in the United States and is especially noted for sending its graduates to elite colleges and universities. Yo-Yo continued his fifth-grade trend of cutting classes.

He spent just a year at The Trinity School before transferring to The Professional Children's School, which was founded in 1914, more than two centuries after The Trinity School. The curriculum of PCS was geared toward young performers. Its alumni over the years have included Scarlett Johansson, Sarah Michelle Gellar, Macauley Culkin, and other well-known actors. But in spite of the accommodating schedule at PCS, Yo-Yo's penchant for cutting classes grew even stronger. Soon his teachers decided that he was bored and put him into an accelerated program. As a result, he graduated from PCS in 1971 when he was just 15.

A few weeks before that, he had given his first solo Carnegie Hall recital. Allen Hughes of the *New York Times* wrote of the performance, "Yo-Yo Ma is said to have been a prodigy when he was a child, and although he is growing older now—he is all of 16 [sic]—one can well believe it. The cello recital he gave at Carnegie Recital Hall Thursday night was of a quality to make many an older man green with envy."[10]

Hughes wasn't the only one who admired the concert. So did Emanuel Ax, a pianist five years older than Yo-Yo. "It was the most incredible exhibition of string playing I've ever heard from such a young player. I was twenty-one at the time, and I vividly remember thinking that I'd like to work with him one day."[11] Ax eventually would work with Yo-Yo, though several years would elapse before the two young men joined forces.

The recital also marked a turning point in Yo-Yo's development. Up to this point, Rose had been guiding Yo-Yo through the music that he played. That was about to change. Shortly after the recital, Rose handed Yo-Yo the score to a Beethoven cello sonata and told him to figure it out for himself. Like the Bach cello suites, it was a very complex piece of music. Yo-Yo struggled with it, and confessed that it took years before he felt that he fully understood it.

"But it was the beginning of my conscious search for independence and individuality," he said. "It takes a great teacher to grant that kind of permission and encouragement."[12]

Another aspect of his "conscious search for independence" took far less time to develop. It manifested itself that summer when he attended a well-known camp for string players called Meadowmount. This long-standing summer camp had been established in 1944 by noted violin teacher Ivan Galamian. It was located in Westport, New York, in the Adirondack Mountains.

More than a century earlier, British novelist Charles Dickens began *A Tale of Two Cities* with the words, "It was the best of times, it was the worst of times." He might have been describing the summer of 1971 for Yo-Yo, who found himself suddenly free to explore his creativity.

"It was my first experience of being among kids who also loved music and wanted to play," he said. "When someone said, 'Come on, let's read some Beethoven quartets at two o'clock in the morning,' I went nuts, it was so exciting."[13] He unleashed his newfound sense of freedom on his cello. "I just started playing my heart out," he said. "You're 15. You've got a lot of feelings inside. From that moment on, it's been a continuing process."[14]

This exuberance impressed his fellow campers. One was violinist Wendy Rose, now a member of the Toronto Symphony. "I heard Yo-Yo playing the Franck sonata, and I burst into tears," she said. "The sheer beauty of his playing was totally overwhelming. I just couldn't stop crying."[15]

On the other hand, it was also the first time that he was away from home and the stern discipline of his father. "I just ran wild, as if I'd been let out of a ghetto," he said. "The whole structure of discipline collapsed. I exploded into bad taste at every level."[16]

He left his cello outside on several occasions, exposing it to the elements. He drank beer. He skipped rehearsals. Perhaps the worst example of this "bad taste" was covering a wall with graffiti having to do with the possible relations between certain male and female campers. He was caught and punished by having to paint over the entire wall.

The rebellion carried over into the fall when he returned to New York City. At his first lesson of the season with Rose, he showed up wearing a leather jacket and mouthing a string of curses. That was a far cry from the timid youngster of several years earlier. Rose took it in stride, still fully believing in Yo-Yo no matter how foul his language.

Soon Yo-Yo had to make an important decision. He still wasn't sure about the direction he wanted his life to take. Many people in his situation would have taken full advantage of their talent and the nurturing that Rose and other teachers had provided and begun a performing career. He would surely have been able to find fulfilling work; orchestras throughout the country routinely featured soloists in their mid-to-late teens.

In some ways, Yo-Yo was facing the same decision as outstanding young basketball players: whether to turn pro as soon as possible and cash in on their ability or play for a college team for several seasons, hone their talent even further, and at the same time develop their social and intellectual skills. According to author Andrew L. Pincus, "[Yo-Yo] has often likened the years between fifteen and twenty to an 'emotional bank account' in which you must draw the rest of your life. You can play a lot of concerts or you can open yourself to learning about the world around you, he says, and thus about yourself. But you can't do both."[17]

Yo-Yo decided to learn about the world around him and began attending Columbia University, located just a few miles from his home. However, living at home and commuting to Columbia did not fulfill Yo-Yo's desire to expand his life experience. He later said that the short trip to Columbia made him feel like he was still in high school. Within a few months he dropped out, but didn't tell his parents. Instead, he spent much of his time at Juilliard, just hanging out and trying to fit in with the other students, many of whom were several years older than he was.

His rebellion got worse. "All I was trying to do was to be accepted as one of the guys, and not be considered a freak,"[18] he said.

One of the things that "the guys" did was to obtain fake IDs and use them to purchase alcohol. Apparently that didn't present a problem for Yo-Yo, who quickly put the forged document to use. He'd often rush out during rehearsal breaks and buy bottles of alcohol to pass around—while reserving a generous portion for himself. Somehow he managed to conceal that part of his life from his parents. But his deception couldn't last forever.

One afternoon his father had assembled the Children's Orchestra for a rehearsal. Hiao-Tsiun expected everyone to arrive promptly. When the starting time of 4:00 came around, everyone was there—except Yo-Yo. The minutes ticked slowly by. Marina was getting more and more worried. For Hiao-Tsiun's son to be late would be very humiliating. She knew that her husband wouldn't make a public spectacle. It would be different when they were at home. Hiao-Tsiun would erupt.

Finally at 4:45, the receptionist at the school where the rehearsal was being held whispered to Marina that she had a phone call. It was one of Yo-Yo's fellow students at Juilliard. He had shocking news: Yo-Yo had just been taken to the emergency room of a nearby hospital.

Yo-Yo's alcohol abuse had finally caught up with him. He began vomiting during a rehearsal at Juilliard, then passed out. Because this was a time of heightened drug use among young people in the United States, Juilliard school authorities assumed that he was suffering from a drug overdose. An overdose could easily become a life-threatening situation, so they immediately called an ambulance. It rushed Yo-Yo to the emergency room at a nearby hospital, where his actual condition was diagnosed. Because he was a minor, his parents had to be notified.

Yo-Yo was thoroughly embarrassed by the incident. He was struggling to become American, but the traditionalism of his Chinese ancestry was still firmly ingrained in him—especially the part about bringing shame on the family. He begged his mother to conceal the incident from his father. Reluctantly, Marina promised that she would.

She quickly had second thoughts. In the tight-knit world of classical music in New York City, it was a virtual certainty that Hiao-Tsiun would eventually learn of the incident. She decided to perform a certain amount of damage control and tell him herself.

She urged her husband not to punish Yo-Yo. That would only make things worse, she said. Instead, she thought that they should confront the problem head-on. She recommended that she and Hiao-Tsiun let their son know that they were embarrassed and disappointed, then leave it up to Yo-Yo to remedy the problem himself.

To make it appear that she hadn't broken her promise to Yo-Yo, they decided on a clever tactic. Hiao-Tsiun would claim that he ran into one of Yo-Yo's fellow musicians. According to the fake story, the musician would have asked Hiao-Tsiun how his son was doing, since the other musician supposedly would not have seen Yo-Yo since the boy was taken to the hospital.

The artful plan for confronting Yo-Yo about his drinking worked. Though it may have been difficult, Hiao-Tsiun restrained his anger. Instead, he adopted a diplomatic approach. "Maybe you don't realize it, Yo-Yo, but I need you at rehearsals, and when you don't show up, the entire orchestra suffers," he explained. "You let the children down, and that is not fair to them."[19]

Yo-Yo got the message. The combination of his father's words and the obvious fact that he had brought shame on the family straightened him out, though the incident had repercussions that in some cases lasted for several more years.

One was that Hiao-Tsiun felt that perhaps he needed to set a better example for his son. For years, one of his few personal indulgences had been enjoying a glass of wine with dinner. In the wake of the incident, he abandoned this custom for four years.

Yo-Yo underwent counseling at Juilliard for a period because Rose felt he was under too much stress. The news of the embarrassing event even crossed the Atlantic to France, where people still remembered the Ma family. "For the next five years," Yo-Yo later recalled, "everywhere I went people would look at me and think, This guy is trouble. When I'd arrive late for a rehearsal, or entirely forgot to come, everybody thought the worst."[20]

But as often happens, something bad can lead to something good. Columbia had not been a good experience, perhaps because the youngster wasn't ready for it. Now he felt that he was ready, although not for Columbia. His sister Yeou-Cheng was attending Radcliffe College, which was located in Cambridge, Massachusetts. Yo-Yo decided to attend Harvard University, just a few blocks away from Radcliffe. He felt that getting an academic education was important, even if it meant delaying his performing career. Isaac Stern later suggested that despite Yo-Yo's defiance of many Chinese traditions, this decision might have reflected his acceptance of one—its respect for the value of learning.

In fact, Yo-Yo wasn't even sure at this point that he wanted to follow a career as a professional musician.

"By that time I had played the cello for a good ten, eleven years, and there was something in me that knew I wasn't ready to go out and play concerts," he explained in an interview. "I knew I was young and immature. I also knew that playing the instrument, even playing it relatively well, was not what music was about. And I knew there were many things about the world that I wanted to know more about."[21]

At this important juncture, he crossed paths with Pablo Casals once again, at the 1972 Marlboro Festival. This festival was founded in 1951 on the campus of Marlboro College in Vermont. It is one of the most prestigious summer programs in classical music. Its hallmark is the opportunity for gifted young musicians to study and to perform concerts with many of the biggest names in the field. It was the first time in a decade that Yo-Yo had been with Casals. The timing was ideal.

"Here was this ninety-year-old man who was practically non-functional," he recalled. "But the second he got on the podium, he was singing, screaming, and yelling. That strength was inspiring. By normal standards he couldn't play the cello [the way he had in earlier years], but the commitment behind each note, the belief, he had, was a wonderful example."[22]

Meeting Casals and other committed musicians would have been ample justification for the time that was involved in attending the festival. But that summer included a meeting that was to prove of even more importance.

NOTES

1. Robert Sherman, "Celebrities Help Ecole Francaise," *New York Times*, December 18, 1964.

2. Ibid.

3. Tim Janof, "Leonard Rose Remembered," http://www.cello.org/Newsletter/Articles/rose/rose.htm.

4. Ibid.

5. David Blum, *Quintet: Five Journeys Toward Musical Fulfillment* (Ithaca, N.Y.: Cornell University Press, 1999), p. 9.

6. Ibid., p. 10.

7 Robert Hatch and William Hatch, *The Hero Project* (New York: McGraw Hill, 2006), p. 78.

8. Marina Ma, as told to John A. Rallo, *My Son, Yo-Yo* (Hong Kong: The Chinese University Press, 1995), p. 99.

9. Pablo Casals, *Joys and Sorrows: His Own Story as Told to Albert E. Kahn* (New York: Simon and Schuster, 1970), p. 43.

10. Allen Hughes, "Yo-Yo Ma, Cellist, Now 16, Performs an Enviable Recital," *New York Times*, May 8, 1971.

11. Blum, *Quintet*, p. 12

12. "Leonard Rose, Cellist," http://www.cello.org/cnc.rose.htm.

13. Edith Eisler, "Yo-Yo Ma as Experimenter, Colleague and Teacher," *Andante* (May 2001), http://andante.com/article/print/cfm?id=12748&varticletype=INTER.

14. Gerri Hirshey, "We Are the World (Cellist Yo-Yo Ma)," *Parade*, January 30, 2005.

15. Ibid.

16. Blum, *Quintet*, p. 11.

17. Andrew L. Pincus, *Musicians with a Mission: Keeping the Classical Tradition Alive* (Boston: Northeastern University Press, 2002), p. 18.

18. Blum, *Quintet*, p. 13.

19. Ma, *My Son, Yo-Yo*, p. 130.

20. Ibid.

21. "From the Top: Radio and Television: Hall of Fame—Yo-Yo Ma," http://www.fromthetop.org/Programs/HallOfFame.cfm?pid=1858.

22. Margaret Campbell, *The Great Cellists* (London: Victor Gallancz, 1988), p. 318.

Chapter 6

LEARNING OF LOVE
AND LOVE OF LEARNING

Several months before the 1972 Marlboro festival Yo-Yo had given a performance at Mount Holyoke, a college in western Massachusetts. On that occasion he met a student named Jill Hornor, a violinist who had played in the Greater Boston Youth Symphony Orchestra. Now she was working in the Marlboro Festival office and Yo-Yo renewed his acquaintance. They soon realized that both had spent substantial portions of their formative years living in Europe, giving them a common sense of background.

For Yo-Yo, Jill had a much more important quality than her background. "She was probably the first person who really wanted to find out what I truly thought," he recalled. "She used to say, 'What do you really mean by that?' That totally dumbfounded me."[1]

By the time the festival ended, he told her that he was falling in love with her. At first she wasn't sure of her feelings. She was beginning her junior year in college while Yo-Yo would just be a freshman—and because of his early graduation from high school, an especially young freshman. She thought of him more as a little brother.

That situation didn't take long to change. Yo-Yo moved up to Cambridge to prepare for the start of his freshman year at Harvard, and began biking back and forth to Jill's home in nearby Brookline. Their romantic relationship quickly budded. But a potential obstacle to the relationship arose soon afterward: Jill left to spend her junior year studying in Paris.

Frequently, separations such as these spell the end of relationships. Not in this case. Yo-Yo found that it was often easier to use letters to convey his feelings rather than saying them to Jill face-to-face. Within a short period of time, they were writing to each other on almost a daily basis, and compiling very high telephone bills in an era before the advent of cheap long-distance calling.

Yo-Yo was far too busy to brood about the fact that he and Jill were so far apart. Harvard is one of the most demanding colleges in the country. He was carrying a full academic load. During his college years he would be taking courses in history, math, science, art, literature, and numerous other subjects.

He devised a unique method of coping with his coursework. Describing himself as "unbelievably lazy in everything," he explained that, "I had very low standards—I didn't feel compelled to get high grades. . . . I worked in spurts. If I could no longer put off writing a paper, I studied into the night."[2]

This approach, of course, had its drawbacks. On one occasion he put off listening to the assigned recordings for a music class he was taking until it was almost too late. He solved that problem by picking the lock on the music library, sneaking inside, and cramming several weeks' worth of listening assignments into a single long night. On another occasion, he overslept, missed a test, and was placed on academic probation. In a particularly ironic lapse, he almost failed music history, which he confessed was "a subject I should have done okay in. I handed papers in late. I think I ended up with a D+."[3]

In his own mind, whatever academic shortcomings he may have had were more than offset by the sheer excitement of learning. He took classes from stimulating professors, but they were not the only source of his excitement.

"I was passionate about what I was doing, and I had classmates who were as passionate about what they were doing as I was,"[4] he explained. He thought nothing of calling his new friends at all hours of the night to discuss the material they were covering in class. To Yo-Yo, his unregulated learning style enabled his overall development. "My generally undisciplined approach to life offers me the possibility of doing many things," he said. "I wanted to try to tie together the various threads of my life."[5]

Some of the most important threads of Yo-Yo's life originated at Harvard, and came full circle there. Nearly three decades after his graduation in 1976, he returned to Harvard to accept the 2004 Harvard Arts Medal. The award is based not just on artistic accomplishment but also the contributions that its recipients have made to the overall benefit of the community around them. Its bestowal is part of a program begun in 1995 by fellow Harvard alumnus and actor John Lithgow called Arts First.

"Without question, everything that I've done in the last ten to twenty years is a direct result of what I was first exposed to in college,"[6] Yo-Yo told

Lithgow as part of a wide-ranging interview in front of a sold-out audience that also had the opportunity to hear him play.

One of the most notable of Yo-Yo's undertakings in his adult years, and which had bearing on his being awarded the Harvard Arts Medal, was a direct result of an anthropology class taught by Irven DeVore, one of the world's leading authorities on the Bushmen of the Kalahari. The Kalahari is the desert that encompasses much of the southwestern African countries of Namibia and Botswana. DeVore planted a seed that would grow to fruition more than two decades later and have a profound effect on Yo-Yo's life.

DeVore had a much more immediate effect. He was a lover of classical music who had listened to Casals on numerous occasions while doing research in Puerto Rico, where Casals made his home during much of his later life. Shortly after Yo-Yo began his studies at Harvard, DeVore attended a concert that Yo-Yo presented on campus. Saying that he was impressed is a considerable understatement. "I want to tell you that last night I heard a Harvard freshman play the cello, and his expertise puts any athlete in the shade, and far exceeds that of the acknowledged master of his field, Pablo Casals," he told his class the following morning. "That freshman is sitting right up there."[7] He pointed to Yo-Yo, who promptly turned purple.

As DeVore's comment indicates, Yo-Yo certainly hadn't turned his back on music while immersing himself in his academic classes. During his first year he was frequently absent on weekends, traveling around the country to perform in concerts. That may have been one reason why he hadn't done particularly well academically.

For the rest of his stay at Harvard, he stayed much closer to home. He soon formed a trio with two other talented musicians whom he had known slightly from their days at The Juilliard School. One was Lynn Chang, a talented violinist who went on to become a frequent soloist. The other was pianist Richard Kogan, who became a noted psychiatrist.

The three of them still get together for occasional concert appearances. When that happens, Ma always inserts his favorite line: "If I ever need psychiatric help, Ricky's the one."[8]

Kogan doubts that Yo-Yo will ever call on his services. "He has of course a healthy narcissism, but there isn't a trace of the pathological narcissism you see in people in his talent category," he says. "If you're looking for Citizen Kane's Rosebud, something to unlock the mystery, I'm not sure there is a lot more than what you see."[9]

In addition to his concerts with Chang and Kogan, Yo-Yo performed frequently on campus and soon made a considerable name for himself. Kogan vividly remembers one concert in particular. It had long been a sellout and hundreds of people thronged the ticket office in the faint hope that they might get a ticket. Hearing of their plight, Yo-Yo came out before the concert started and played Bach suites for them until a few moments before the curtain went up.

His relationship with Jill proved to be as successful as his concerts. The year she spent apart from him in Paris had only made them closer. Yet when she returned to the United States, they were still separated geographically. She went to graduate school at Cornell University in Ithaca, New York, several hundred miles from Harvard. Though they were still physically apart, Yo-Yo regarded the separation as a plus. "Paradoxically, the fact that we had rarely been in the same city at the same time allowed us to get to know each other better," he said. "The breathing space also permitted us to develop on our own."[10]

Chang points out one particularly successful area of Yo-Yo's personal development. "He [Yo-Yo] was just so shy at the beginning," he recalled. "By the end of four years he was much more outgoing—he just opened up. More than what he gleaned academically, he gleaned the most from how to communicate and interpersonal relationships."[11]

Of course, Yo-Yo also developed musically. He attributes much of that development to three professors he had at Harvard. One was Luise Vosgerchian, who also served as pianist with the Boston Symphony Orchestra. She encouraged him to study a musical score analytically, helping him to determine the elements that gave it its particular flavor and to see it from the point of view of the entire orchestra, rather than simply the cello.

Patricia Zander was the second. Also a pianist, she had told him bluntly after one of his early Harvard concerts that in her view he simply didn't know what he was doing. She didn't mean to be harsh; she simply felt that he was capable of doing better. The two of them soon began playing together and eventually gave a number of public performances, sometimes flying thousands of miles from separate locations in order to do so.

Perhaps Yo-Yo's most influential Harvard instructor was Leon Kirchner, who was a composer in addition to his teaching duties. While Yo-Yo learned a great deal from Kirchner, the man was often hard on him.

"I was always telling Yo-Yo that he didn't have the true center of his tone yet," Kirchner said, "meaning there was something more spiritual, the center of his person, of his being, that was not coming through yet."[12]

This lack of "true center" became even more apparent in 1976, not long before Yo-Yo's graduation, when noted Russian cellist Mstislav Rostropovich paid a visit to Harvard to conduct a master class.

To many musicians, Rostropovich had taken on Casals' mantle as the world's greatest cellist. The comparison was particularly apt because he had a tangible connection with Casals. The great master had taught Rostropovich's father, who then taught his son to play the cello when he was 10.

Rostropovich had another connection to Casals: he was as passionately devoted to human freedom and artistic expression as Casals had been. This sometimes got him into trouble with Soviet authorities, who felt that the arts should be at the service of the state. At about the same time that Yo-Yo was rebelling against his father's demands, Rostropovich was fighting an even more formidable foe—the leadership of the Soviet Union.

His friend Aleksandr Solzhenitsyn had written scathing portrayals of the Gulag, the notorious forced labor prison system in the Soviet Union, for which he was awarded the Nobel Prize for Literature in 1970. Soviet authorities were outraged at being "outed." Rostropovich showed his personal courage by allowing Solzhenitsyn to live with him for several years. He also sent a letter to Western newspapers that was openly critical of the way in which arts were administered in the Soviet Union.

The consequences were harsh. Rostropovich wasn't allowed to travel outside his country, and many of his concerts inside the Soviet Union were canceled. In 1974 Soviet authorities granted him a two-year exit visa, which effectively exiled him from his native country. He and his family came to the United States, where he was welcomed with open arms.

Before his Harvard visit, Rostropovich asked Kirchner for a list of his top five students. Yo-Yo was at the top. Now Rostropovich was facing a young man whose talents had been favorably compared with his.

Unlike his first meeting with Casals more than a decade earlier, this time Yo-Yo was thoroughly familiar with the musicianship of the man he was facing. He had heard a recording of Rostropovich playing the Shostakovich Cello Concerto No. 1 in E flat major several years earlier, and it had left an indelible impression. "That recording just made my hair stand on end," he said. "I couldn't sleep that night."[13]

Rostropovich's master class at Harvard was conducted in front of an audience. As Kirchner described the scene, "When Yo-Yo began playing for [Rostropovich], he stopped him and said, 'You know you have no center to your tone.' The audience was not happy with this criticism of Yo-Yo, but they didn't understand that Rostropovich, too, recognized that here was something very different, something worthy of the deepest criticism."[14]

The criticism made a definite impact on Yo-Yo. "Boy, he took no prisoners," he recalled. "He immediately zeroed in on my weaknesses and proved to me that I didn't know what was happening in the score even though I was trying to wiggle out of admitting it, and basically it's one of those things where someone comes in to your life and tells you the things that other people have been telling you but because it's that person it makes you pay attention much more."[15]

Both men emerged from the encounter with a great deal of respect for each other. The following year Rostropovich, who had just been appointed as conductor of the National Symphony Orchestra in Washington, D.C., invited Yo-Yo to appear with the orchestra as a soloist.

By that time, Yo-Yo was starting to feel that he had to do something definite regarding Jill. A violinist friend, Heiichiro Ohyama, told him in essence to fish or cut bait. "If you don't do something, fish swim away,"[16] Ohyama said. While Yo-Yo hardly looked at Jill as a "fish," he got the point.

He and Ohyama worked out a plan. Yo-Yo went to New York City. He called Jill and told her to be home at seven o'clock that evening, then hopped on board a bus to Ithaca. Promptly at seven he called her from a nearby phone booth and asked her if she missed him. She assured him that she did. In less than a minute, she heard her doorbell ring. She opened the door to see Yo-Yo Ma standing there, wearing his best suit.

He dropped to his knees. "Will you marry me?" he asked.

"I can't believe this!" she shrieked. "Yes, sure!"[17]

Yo-Yo slipped the wedding ring he had purchased that morning onto her finger, then told her to pack. He had also bought two plane tickets to visit her parents in Cleveland, who happily gave their blessing.

Blessings did not come so easily from Yo-Yo's parents, especially his father. Hiao-Tsiun had nothing against Jill personally. But she was not Chinese, and he wanted his son to marry a Chinese woman in keeping with tradition. Hiao-Tsiun and Marina believed that marrying a Westerner might cause Yo-Yo, and especially Yo-Yo's children, to turn away from their Chinese heritage. Eventually Hiao-Tsiun and Marina were able to overcome their objections and welcome Jill into the family.

Yo-Yo and Jill were married on May 20, 1978. About a week and a half earlier, Yo-Yo had received a much-appreciated "wedding gift": the Avery Fisher Prize.

The award is named for Avery Fisher, who donated the money to fund it. Fisher was born in Brooklyn in 1906, and he graduated from New York University in 1929. He went to work as a book designer, but it was a low-paying job. "I felt that the only way to better myself was to do something else," he recalled many years later.[18]

Fortunately for him—and for countless numbers of music lovers—he didn't have to search far for that "something else." Music was his real passion. He loved playing his violin, though he had no intention of trying to become a professional. Frustrated by the relatively poor sound quality of both radios and record players of the era, he decided to create improved systems that would bring the joy he felt in listening to music to as many people as possible.

Fisher began experimenting with these improvements in his spare time. His tinkering didn't take long to produce results. In 1937 he established his own company, Philharmonic Radio, which produced radios with enhanced sound quality. An article in *Fortune* magazine about him and his company entitled "The Golden Ear" appeared a year later and helped the fledgling company get off the ground.

Fisher moved into high gear at the end of World War II in 1945. He sold Philharmonic Radio and began a second company, Fisher Radio. It made even better products, in part because he hired outstanding sound engineers from Europe. Many of them leaped at the chance to escape the economic and physical devastation that had engulfed the European continent and obtain high-paying jobs in the United States.

A little over a decade later, his efforts began paying off. He introduced the first amplifier that used a relatively new invention, the transistor. Then he invented the first combination stereophonic radio and phonograph. He continued with his innovations, and also positioned his company at the high end of sound quality. His products were regarded as the Rolls Royce of sound systems. (Rolls Royce was a manufacturer of premium automobiles and a byword for quality in that era.) This business strategy made him a very wealthy man, and he became even richer when he sold Fisher Radio to the Emerson Company in 1969.

By then, Fisher had acquired a reputation as a philanthropist, particularly in the area of classical music. In 1973, he donated more than $10 million to the New York Philharmonic to help remodel Philharmonic Hall because of an increasing recognition that its acoustics needed to be improved. The venue was renamed Avery Fisher Hall to honor him.

Fisher also wanted to encourage the people who made the music that would now sound so much better in the renovated hall. So in 1974 he established the Avery Fisher Artist Program. It consisted of two parts: the Avery Fisher Career Grants and the Avery Fisher Prize. Under the program's terms, several Career Grants would be awarded each year to help up-and-coming musicians. The grants provide funding and recognition to help them advance their careers.

The Avery Fisher Prize is even more prestigious than the Avery Career Grant. It goes to outstanding young instrumental players who appear to be on the cusp of particularly distinguished careers.

The prize was awarded for the first time in 1975, when pianist Murray Perahia and cellist Lynn Harrell (who had also studied with Leonard Rose) shared it. It wasn't awarded in 1976 and 1977, so Yo-Yo became its third recipient. Then as now, the award includes a tax-free cash prize, which in 2007 was $75,000; but far more important is the prestige that accompanies it. The recipients are marked as significant musicians and are guaranteed performances with the New York Philharmonic. Some people even regard the Avery Fisher Prize as the Oscar of classical music.

There is, however, one major difference between the Avery Fisher and the Oscar. Fisher took no part in naming the award winners, but he established the criteria used to determine them. He made it clear that he was adamantly opposed to any form of open competition. Consequently, musicians cannot apply for the awards. Nor are the musicians under consideration aware that they are being scrutinized by the committee that makes the determination.

In another sense, however, the Oscar analogy applies. Frequently the Academy Award ceremonies include a Lifetime Achievement Award, given for the recipient's accomplishments in the film industry over the course of his or her career. Similarly, the Avery Fisher Prize committee closely examines what any musician under consideration has done so far in addition to evaluating the musician's talent—though of course "so far" encompasses just a handful of years in comparison with the Lifetime Achievement Oscar, which spans decades.

"We want someone with a proven capacity, musically and technically, to maintain a sustained career," explains a member of the committee. "Beyond that, it's a little tricky. The person must be mature enough and old enough to have demonstrated this, yet young enough to be classified as a young musician."[19]

The committee's standards are exacting. Since Yo-Yo's award in 1978, only 16 musicians have been deemed worthy to win it, and five of those were honored in 1999 and 2000. There was a four-year span (1995–1998) when no one measured up.

With the prestige of the Avery Fisher Prize buoying his reputation, it quickly became obvious that Yo-Yo Ma was on the move. Soon after his marriage, he embarked on a grueling performance schedule.

One of these performances was at the Spoleto Festival USA in Charleston, South Carolina, where he demonstrated the sense of humor that is one of his most pronounced characteristics. During a rehearsal for a Ravel chamber composition, harpist Heidi Lehwalder noticed that the notes she was playing for her solo part didn't sound right. Moments later she realized why: Yo-Yo was leaning over and quietly moving some of the seven pedals on her instrument with his feet.

Several weeks later the same musicians were in Italy for the Spoleto Festival. Both festivals had been founded by composer Gian Carlo Menotti (best known for the opera *Amahl and the Night Visitors*) to showcase the talents of rising young musicians. On a lark Yo-Yo decided to wear a nineteenth-century Chinese queue when he played a cello solo. The long ponytail was in constant motion during his performance. The stern-faced Menotti was sitting only a few feet away in the audience.

"I don't think I should have done that,"[20] Yo-Yo said when he came offstage.

"He's such a free spirit," Lehwalder said later. "It was six weeks of a lot of fun. And I beat him in arm-wrestling!"[21]

When Yo-Yo wasn't on the road, he and Jill lived on the Harvard campus. She worked as a German tutor, while Yo-Yo was artist in residence. Sometimes his tasks were formal, such as tutoring cello students and teaching occasional classes. At other times, they were informal, such as the time that he and Jill hosted a waltz party. Yo-Yo was content to join student musicians and play Strauss waltzes far into the night.

But just when it appeared that the forward thrust of Yo-Yo's burgeoning career was unstoppable, nature stepped in and threatened to bring it to a crashing halt.

NOTES

1. Janet Tassel, "Yo-Yo Ma's Journeys," *Harvard Magazine*, March–April 2000, http://www.harvardmagazine.com/on-line/0300127.html.

2. David Blum, *Quintet: Five Journeys Toward Musical Fulfillment* (Ithaca, N.Y.: Cornell University Press, 1999), p. 14.

3. "Arts First: An Evening With Yo-Yo Ma," http://athome.harvard.edu/programs/yym/.

4. Ibid.

5. Blum, *Quintet*, p. 14.

6. "Arts First."

7. Tassel, "Yo-Yo Ma's Journeys."

8. Evan Eisenberg, "MUSIC: Through College and Life, in Harmony," *New York Times*, July 15, 2001.

9. Tassel, "Yo-Yo Ma's Journeys."

10. Blum, *Quintet*, p. 18.

11. Sara A. Dolgonos and Amit R. Paley, "College Taught Ma to Play His Own Tune." *Harvard Crimson*, June 5, 2001, http://www.thecrimson.com/article.aspx?ref=104513.

12. Ibid.

13. "Yo Yo Ma Reflects on Rostropovich," *All Things Considered*, National Public Radio, April 27, 2007, http://www.npr.org/templates/story/story. php?storyId=9884094.

14. Tassel, "Yo-Yo Ma's Journeys."

15. "Yo Yo Ma Reflects on Rostropovich," *All Things Considered*.

16. Blum, *Quintet*, p. 18.

17. Ibid., p. 19.

18. Allan Kozinn, "A Benefactor Tells Why He Did It," *New York Times*, March 2, 1986.

19. Ibid.

20. Heidi Lehwalder, personal interview with the author, February 19, 2008.

21. Ibid.

Chapter 7

CAST-CLAD, BECOMING A DAD, AND A NEW STRAD

"Jill signed on to a wreck,"[1] Yo-Yo told Gerri Hirshey of *Parade* magazine, referring to one aspect of his physical condition at the time of their marriage.

Known medical cases of problems like Yo-Yo's "wreck" actually dated back at least 2,500 years. Hippocrates, the ancient Greek who is widely considered to be the father of Western medicine, recorded having diagnosed a condition involving the spinal column that he called scoliosis. He derived the name from a Greek word meaning *crooked*. Yo-Yo's spine was very crooked indeed.

Normally, the spinal column is vertical (when viewed from the rear; scoliosis is not to be confused with the normal spinal curve as seen from the side). As children grow, their spines sometimes curve toward the left or the right. In more severe cases, this curvature assumes an "S" shape, bending twice. No one knows why scoliosis occurs. Nor does anyone know why this condition is much more common among females than among males.

In the majority of cases, the curvature isn't serious enough to require any action, though physicians usually monitor the degree of deviation closely. If the curvature exceeds 30 degrees, however, the situation changes. At this point, the next step is usually to apply some sort of bracing to influence the spine toward normal development. If curvature continues to worsen, surgery may be called for. The best time for an operation is during adolescence, while the patient's bones are continuing to grow.

Yo-Yo had long since passed both parameters—for the optimal age for surgery and for excessive curvature. Over the years, his spine had developed a pronounced S-curve. One bend was 63 degrees, while the other was 67. Not only did the severe bending result in physical deformity, it threatened a much more serious condition: reducing the available volume of space in his chest for his heart and lungs.

He was also considering surgery belatedly. At the age of 24, he was obviously no adolescent. He had been aware of his scoliosis for some time, but he had understandably been reluctant to halt his career for the months of down time that would be necessary to correct it. Now he had nearly reached the point of no return. He had to deal with the situation in the brief window of time that was still available to him before his bones finally stopped growing and became static.

The procedure to correct severe scoliosis is complicated. It involves the insertion of steel rods, held in place by rivets, to stretch the spine and straighten it out. Then the surgeon adds grafts from the patient's pelvic bone. This grafting sets off a growth process in which the spine becomes fused. That is why it is essential to do the procedure while the patient is still young: his or her bones are still developing and responsive to the stimulus to grow.

The surgery carries a substantial amount of risk. Many nerves radiate outward from the spine, which means significant damage to those nerves can occur during an operation. If nerve damage occurred, Yo-Yo wouldn't be able to play the cello—or he could suffer even worse. There was a very small but nevertheless very real possibility of complete paralysis.

"Jill knew of the risk before we were married, and she had faith in me even if it turned out that I couldn't continue playing,"[2] he said. "I remember thinking, 'OK, if I never play the cello again, I'm fine.' In some ways, it was freeing. Because you kind of say, 'Well, OK, done that,' and move on."[3]

Before going under the knife, Yo-Yo considered his alternatives. "I had decided that there's more to life than the cello," he said. "There are so many things that I would find enormously exciting. I love people; perhaps I'd do social work, or become a teacher."[4]

Whatever he chose, he relished the thought that he would be able to go back to school, to regain the enthusiasm for learning that had inspired him eight years earlier when he began his studies at Harvard. He would be in no hurry to make up his mind as to a major; he'd simply take classes until he found something that resonated with him, something that he would feel passionate about.

As things turned out, he didn't have to face such a choice. The operation was successful. Now he faced the necessity of being in an upper-body cast for six months to keep his spine absolutely rigid and to allow the bones to have ample time to fuse. The doctors configured the cast so he could continue to play his cello.

Yo-Yo's typical good nature was apparent when the operation was over. "With my cast on, I felt like a football player," he explained. "I had broad shoulders, a fabulous physique. I thought I could walk through the most dangerous slum of any city and nobody would dare attack me."[5]

The operation had other benefits. For one, the pressure of meeting dozens of concert dates was removed while he was in the cast. Consequently, he had a great deal of unaccustomed free time to spend with Jill. The two of them went hiking and did other things together that normally would have been precluded by his busy schedule.

The enforced quiet also gave him time to think about his relationship with his father. In particular, he began to understand some of the reasons for the extreme degree of discipline his father had imposed on him. "After all my years of rebellion, I recently was able to thank him for creating boulders for me to overcome," he said. "Without them, I never would have found my identity."[6]

Not every matter surrounding Yo-Yo's surgery and recovery was so serious. By coincidence, during the same time period, cellist Leonard Rose had fallen while jogging and had broken his collar bone. The two men, now temporarily disabled, spent considerable amounts of time together. The interlude may have been particularly beneficial for Rose.

"He [Rose] never allowed himself to relax, except when he was with Casals, and I never saw him be gregarious except when he was with Yo-Yo," his daughter Barbara recalled. "I remember them sitting in our backyard, surrounded by hedges, commiserating with each other about their condition, and my father would tell story after story, not all of them clean."[7]

This interlude of off-color storytelling with his mentor came to an end when Yo-Yo emerged from his cast. Social work and education's loss was the music world's gain: the operation proved a complete success. With the curves straightened out Yo-Yo actually added two inches to his height. As befit his jovial nature, he turned the event into an opportunity for a joke, telling people he had "grown in stature."

Once Yo-Yo recovered, he found himself even more in demand by the performing world. His management company kept calling—sometimes even when he and Jill were trying to have a calm sit-down dinner—with still more concert dates. Yo-Yo found it almost impossible to say no. But saying yes, of course, meant he actually had to play all those concerts he'd agreed to. In the years immediately after the operation, his yearly roster of performing dates numbered as many as 150—an average of three a week. This schedule posed enormous physical demands.

"Playing any acoustic instrument in a large hall is strenuous," Yo-Yo said. "A lot of cellists end up with back problems or tendonitis. I do aerobics, weights, all that stuff to insulate against the short nights and cramped airplanes."[8]

Transportation to and from the various performing venues was even more taxing. One concert at about this time, at Bowling Green University in Ohio, illustrates a typical scenario. Yo-Yo drove from his home near the Harvard campus to the Boston airport, met his playing partner Patricia Zander (with whom he had studied at Harvard), and flew to Detroit. They rented a car at the airport and drove two hours to the concert site. Upon their arrival in mid-afternoon, both immediately began rehearsing until the start of the concert. The two musicians could not leave once the concert ended; they appeared at a meet-and-greet session that lasted until after 11:00 that night, after which they grabbed a quick meal, drove back to Detroit, and slept a few hours at a hotel near the airport. Early the next morning they took a plane back to Boston. Even then neither could rest. Zander headed for Harvard and her teaching responsibilities, while Yo-Yo had a rehearsal at 10:30 that morning.

This hectic schedule at times created difficult situations that Yo-Yo defused with humor. One such situation occurred in Germany when he and Zander were driving to an evening concert date in Frankfurt. The plan for the morning after the concert was that they would fly to London so Yo-Yo could record the two Haydn cello concertos with Jose Luis Garcia and the English Chamber Orchestra. Unfortunately the car they had rented to transport themselves to Frankfurt that night blew out a tire. Zander set out on foot to get help. Yo-Yo calmly pulled out his cello, sat on one of their suitcases, and began practicing the concertos he was to record the next day. "When you hear that recording you should see asphalt,"[9] he joked.

This overwhelming schedule made burnout a real possibility for Yo-Yo. And the demands on his time became even greater as he began developing his recording career.

His first two recordings had been released in 1979, shortly before his operation. One was a recording of Gerald Finzi's Concerto for Cello and Orchestra, on the Lyrita label, with Vernon Handley conducting the Royal Philharmonic Orchestra. The other was somewhat unusual. Entitled *Robert White Sings Beethoven*, it included a number of Beethoven's least-known works: settings of folk songs from Wales, Scotland, and Ireland. White, a noted tenor, was the featured performer. His singing was accompanied by a threesome consisting of Yo-Yo, violinist Ani Kavafian, and pianist Samuel Sanders.

Yo-Yo's participation was especially noteworthy since he had agreed to do the recording just three months *after* winning the Avery Fisher prize. It was not dissimilar to an actor winning an Oscar in a starring role and then accepting a bit part in his next film.

In retrospect, the album also may have marked the formal beginning of Yo-Yo's willingness to go well beyond the traditional cello literature and explore other forms of music. This willingness would become even more pronounced within a decade.

His management company, International Creative Management (ICM), wasn't happy with his decision to do *Robert White Sings Beethoven*. But even though Yo-Yo was just 23 when he recorded it, he was already willing to stand up for himself.

Presumably management was far more pleased with the two recordings of his that were issued the following year. One, Beethoven's Triple Concerto, was on the Deutsche Grammophon label. Yo-Yo of course played the cello part, while Mark Zeltser was the piano soloist and Anne-Sophie Mutter the violinist. They were under the baton of the renowned conductor Herbert von Karajan. Von Karajan's reputation extended throughout the classical music universe. When he died in 1989 the *New York Times* maintained that in all likelihood he was the world's most famous classical conductor. The cover photo for the album shows von Karajan surrounded by the three soloists, whose combined ages were considerably lower than the maestro's own 71.

Working with such a person as von Karajan was wonderful, yet could be costly. Von Karajan was a formidable presence who commanded profound respect. On one occasion, Yo-Yo was in London. He had just finished a series of concerts there and was resting before taking a commercial flight to Lucerne, Switzerland, for several performances with von Karajan.

"All of a sudden Karajan calls in the middle of the night and schedules a rehearsal for 10 o'clock the next morning," he recalled. "You don't say no to Herbert von Karajan so I frantically chartered a small jet to Zurich and arranged for a car to Lucerne. When we landed, I found that Karajan had changed his mind and had cancelled the rehearsal. It cost me around $4,000."[10]

The second important recording of that year launched Yo-Yo's ongoing career with the CBS Masterworks label (and thereafter with Sony Classical when Sony bought out CBS in 1990): Camille Saint-Saëns' Concerto No. 1 for Cello and Orchestra and Edouard Lalo's Concerto for Cello and Orchestra, with conductor Lorin Maazel and the Orchestra National de France.

Maazel was on virtually the same plane of prestige as von Karajan; he conducted the NBC Symphony Orchestra when he was just seven years old and later served with distinction as the music director of the Cleve-

land Orchestra for more than a decade. He was also named an Ambassador of Good Will by the United Nations.

Being associated with these two first-rank conductors made it apparent
that Yo-Yo was definitely among the world's top-rated cellists. He made
three more recordings in the next two years, and the year after that—
1983—became one of the most significant in his life.

The primary reason was the birth of his son Nicholas. "When you have
your first child, everything changes," he said. "You realize that life is fi-
nite, and that you absolutely have to a limit to your energy. You give, you
love, you care, and it's all different."[11]

One of the main things that was different was the realization that he
needed to set aside time for his family. He quickly learned how to say no
when ICM offered him concert dates. In particular, he refused to accept
anything that conflicted with his children's birthdays. He also set aside an
entire month during the summer to devote to his family.

Another significant event that year was the acquisition of a noteworthy
cello, a 1733 instrument from the Venice workshop of noted luthier Domenico Montagnana. (Up to that point, Yo-Yo had been playing a cello
made in 1722 by Matteo Goffriller.) Montagnana was especially noted
for his cellos and many are still in use today. While Yo-Yo's Montagnana
would make headlines 16 years later, at this time there was little drama
connected with it.

The same couldn't be said of another cello he acquired later that year.
This one bore the most famous name in stringed instruments: Antonio
Stradivari.

As noted cellist Carlos Prieto observes, "Antonio Stradivari represents
the highest point in the history of violinmaking. No one has ever surpassed the sheer quality of the tone, beauty, and perfect craftsmanship of
his instruments."[12] It's only logical that a contemporary magazine devoted
to stringed instruments is named *The Strad*.

Though no birth records exist, it's likely that Stradivari was born in
1644. He wasn't the first of the distinguished Italian luthiers. That distinction belongs to Andrea Amati, who spawned an industry that soon
spread throughout northern Italy and produced thousands of instruments
that are still highly prized today among both musicians and collectors.

This industry reached its peak with Stradivari. The first clue to his professional life comes with the production of his first violin. Its label reads:
"Antonius Stradivarius Cremonesis Alumnus Nicolaii Amati, Faciebat
Anno 1666." Translated, it says that he lived in Cremona and was a pupil
of Nicolò Amati, the grandson of the family business's founder.

The label may be misleading. No firm evidence exists to document that Stradivari ever worked for Amati. Consequently, there's at least a suggestion that Stradivari was a canny marketer who had no hesitation in trying to sell his wares by associating them with the best-known name in the business. The complete absence of the Amati name on Stradivari's subsequent output could mean that Nicolò Amati quickly discovered Stradivari's stratagem and ordered the brash young man to cease and desist.

Not long afterward, Stradivari became established on his own. Thus began a career that led to many innovations in instrument design, though it seems to have required an unhappy personal event to really push Stradivari's star into orbit. His first wife died in 1698 and the 50-year-old Stradivari soon remarried. Perhaps he felt rejuvenated, for almost immediately afterward, according to author Toby Faber, "So began the 'golden period,' when Stradivari's drive for perfection led to the violins, and later cellos, that remain the most highly prized in the world."[13]

The onset of this golden period was also the onset of one of the music world's most enduring mysteries. Stradivari, who continued to work hard into his 90s, didn't leave behind any written documents that would reveal the process he used to create the unique tone of his instruments. He used the same raw materials as his competitors, yet somewhere in his craftsmanship is an X-factor that sets him apart from the others. Experts have carefully examined the Stradivari instruments that have survived the centuries, but the search is complicated by the passage of time, which has undoubtedly wrought some changes in the chemical composition of the wood of which the instruments are made.

The experts have, of course, posited theories. One is that Stradivari coated the wood with pozzolana, a type of fine volcanic dust that hardened the wood and made it waterproof, after which he applied the customary coats of varnish. Another theory is that he covered the wood with a type of fungus that broke down its enzymes. This process would change the texture of the wood and result in subtle changes in tone. A third is that he soaked his wood in salt water. Despite the use of modern technologies such as X-ray diffraction, spectrometers, acoustic tests, and dendrochronological analysis, researchers have been unable to reach any definitive conclusions about the reasons for the excellence of Stradivari's work.

Whatever his secret, Stradivari took it to the grave with him when he died in 1737. That proved to be unfortunate for the men who took over for him. Within a short period of time, they went out of business because musicians were disappointed with what they produced without Stradivari looking over their shoulders. But one thing is certain: In the first decades of the eighteenth century, his company was flourishing. It was during this period—in 1712—that he produced the cello that would come Yo-Yo's way more than 270 years later.

Very little is known of this cello's history until 1843. By that time it had been purchased by Russian nobleman Count Mateusz Wielhorski, who paid for it with a Guarneri cello (made by another notable Cremona family of luthiers), his prize stud horse, and $200,000—a staggering amount of money in that era. Wielhorski was a gifted cellist himself; famed composers such as Felix Mendelssohn and Robert Schumann wrote music for him and praised his accomplishments. Stradivari instruments customarily bear the names of their most prominent users. This one might have been named for Wielhorski, but he was eclipsed by the fame of a subsequent owner: Karl Davidov.

Like Yo-Yo, Davidov was a child prodigy who deferred a musical career to get a university education. Davidov's intention was to become a composer rather than a performer. But when he filled in for another cellist at short notice and was well received, he decided to focus on his playing career. By the early 1860s, he was the object of rave reviews. Peter Tchaikovsky called him the "Czar of Cellos."[14] Fellow cellist Julius Klengel said, "I only understood what cello playing signifies after hearing Davidov in St. Petersburg in my youth."[15]

Clearly, Davidov needed a cello that would match his talent. Wielhorski, by now well advanced in years, decided to give his precious instrument to Davidov, with whose name the instrument was associated from that point on. With its help, Davidov continued to enjoy a distinguished career, though he had to flee Russia in 1887 when he was caught having an affair with one of his students. He returned two years later but became ill while performing and died within a few days.

Davidov's heirs sold the cello to Gabriel Goupillat, a French amateur cellist, in 1900. Goupillat's brother eventually sold it to W. E. Hill & Sons, an English luthier firm. By the 1920s, the boom in the stock market was creating huge fortunes in the United States. Wealthy Americans were always looking for new ways of investing their money—such as purchasing valuable musical instruments.

In 1928 the Davidov Strad attracted front-page headlines when it crossed the Atlantic after being purchased by the Rudolf Wurlitzer Company, one of this country's leading instrument dealers. Befitting an instrument of its lofty pedigree, the cello spent the voyage in the captain's cabin rather than in the cargo hold. Macy's department store heir Herbert N. Straus quickly purchased the instrument from Wurlitzer. While Straus allowed it to be used in occasional chamber music concerts in his home, it was placed in storage after his death. In 1964, Straus's widow asked the Wurlitzer Company to sell the instrument for her. This request dovetailed perfectly with a situation on the other side of the Atlantic Ocean. Jacqueline du Pré needed another cello.

Born in 1945 in England, du Pré was on the cusp of a brilliant career even though she was still a teenager. Her talent was closely akin to Yo-Yo's in a number of respects.

"Jacqueline could sing in tune before she could talk and at three she heard the cello on a Children's Hour programme on the BBC and announced that she wanted 'one of those,'"[16] notes author Margaret Campbell. Little Jacqueline's wish was granted on her next birthday, when she received a full-size cello. The following year she began serious lessons. She made her first public appearance at age 7. Four years later she won a major international cello competition. When she was 16, she gave her first recital and immediately came to the attention of the music community. That timing was almost identical with Yo-Yo's, who had been 15 when he gave his initial recital.

Like Yo-Yo, du Pré had an outgoing, effervescent personality. In fact, her nickname among her fellow musicians was "Smiley." In words that could just as easily have been written about Yo-Yo at a similar age, Elizabeth Wilson said, "Her concerts remain emblazoned in memory as events of uplifting excitement and great festive spirit. With her irresistible, magnetic personality du Pré communicated her emotions with that boundless youthful confidence and vigour which rejoiced in the moment itself."[17]

Indeed, du Pré may have even surpassed Yo-Yo in the degree of her showmanship. Numerous critics noted that she was virtually a force of nature. Certainly her performances remained etched in the memories of her listeners long after the final notes had faded away. As journalist Jessica Duchen noted, "Her bow gouging into the cello string, her long, red-gold hair flying around her silk-clad shoulders, she played with an uninhibited physicality that could conjure up extremes of elemental ferocity and tenderness."[18]

At the point that the Davidov went on the market, du Pré already had one Strad, a 1673 instrument that had been a gift from her godmother, Isména Holland. Because of her aggressive playing style, she wanted another instrument to relieve the stress on her primary cello.

She had already tried and rejected several instruments. The chance to obtain the Davidov came at a perfect moment. Her godmother quickly purchased it for her. Du Pré didn't waste any time putting it to good use; she recorded the Elgar Cello Concerto the following year in a performance that even today is considered definitive.

Three years later her already bright star became incandescent. She married the young Israeli conductor Daniel Barenboim in what was probably the most noteworthy coupling in classical music. Both were young, energetic, attractive, and highly charismatic. The marriage as a whole proved even greater than the sum of its already spectacular parts; the couple often attracted the same sorts of headlines that were associated with rock stars. Du Pré seemed destined for as brilliant a career as would soon be predicted for Yo-Yo.

That career was not to be. In a cruel and ironic coincidence, very close to the time of Yo-Yo's inaugural solo recital in May, 1971, du Pré began to notice the symptoms of a mysterious malady. Her fingers became numb—a catastrophic condition for a string player. She had to cancel numerous concerts and made her final recording that December. Two years later, she faced the cold harsh truth. She had multiple sclerosis. She could no longer play the cello.

Shortly thereafter, the Labour Party came to power in Britain. Du Pré quickly sent the Davidov to Paris so it couldn't be taxed by a government seeking new sources of revenue. It wound up in the storeroom of luthier Etienne Vatelot—the very same man who had built Yo-Yo's first cello—where it languished for nearly a decade.

Then, in 1983, Yo-Yo was given the opportunity to play the instrument, for "fifteen glorious minutes."[19] That was all it took. Yo-Yo "had received his first cello lesson, aged four, in Etienne Vatelot's shop, sitting on three telephone directories," Toby Faber notes. "It seems appropriate that he should have fallen in love with the Davidov under the Frenchman's aegis."[20]

Du Pré and Barenboim decided to lend it to him and he gratefully accepted the offer. Within a short time, he bestowed a nickname on it: "Sweetie Pie."

His Montagnana had also acquired an affectionate moniker. As Yo-Yo explained, "I was doing a class in Salt Lake City, and a high school student asked if I had a nickname for my cello. I said, 'No, but if I play for you, will you name it?' She chose Petunia, and it stuck."[21]

Since that time, the Montagnana and the Strad have been Yo-Yo's primary instruments. He uses a wine analogy to compare them: "The Strad has a tenor quality; it's a Bordeaux, while the Montagnana—big, full, and massive—is a Burgundy. Just as a fine wine leaves a distinctive aftertaste, the Strad leaves a reverberation; its overtones linger for a moment after the bow leaves the string."[22]

In the midst of the many exciting changes in his life—his new son, acquiring the two magnificent cellos, and his demanding concert schedule—Yo-Yo also managed to find the time for three recordings. One was with the legendary Philadelphia Orchestra and its equally legendary music director Eugene Ormandy: cello concertos by the twentieth-century Russian composers Dmitri Shostakovich and Dmitri Kabalevsky. The second recording contained three sonatas for cello and harpsichord by Bach, in collaboration with Kenneth Cooper.

The third recording was the crown jewel: Bach's six cello suites. In a sense, the recording represented a full circle in Yo-Yo's artistic development. It was the same music that his father had assigned him when he was of preschool age, nearly three decades earlier. At that time, the suites marked his first tentative steps into the musical world. Now they represented the mastery of his chosen instrument.

Making this particular album at this point in his career was an act of musical daring. Pablo Casals, even though he was responsible for the prestige and popularity of the suites among cellists, didn't try to record them for the first 35 years following his discovery. Rostropovich was in his 60s before he did so. Yet Yo-Yo wasn't even 30.

To a number of critics, Yo-Yo's relative youthfulness didn't seem to matter. For example, Allan Kozinn of the *New York Times* wrote, "It will undoubtedly be difficult, even for Mr. Ma, to surpass his newly released traversal of Bach's six Suites for Unaccompanied Cello. These are truly magical performances in which the young cellist transcends the characteristics and limitations of his instrument and creates textures that are— unbelievably—nearly orchestral."[23]

NOTES

1. Gerri Hirshey, "We Are the World (Cellist Yo-Yo Ma)," *Parade*, January 30, 2005, http://www.parade.com/articles/editions/2005/edition_01-30-2005/featured_0.

2. David Blum, *Quintet: Five Journeys Toward Musical Fulfillment* (Ithaca, N.Y.: Cornell University Press, 1999), p. 21.

3. Hirshey, "We Are the World."

4. Blum, *Quintet*, p. 22.

5. Ibid., p. 21.

6. Leslie Rubinstein, "Oriental Musicians Come of Age," *New York Times*, November 23, 1980.

7. Tim Janof, "Leonard Rose Remembered," http://www.cello.org/Newsletter/Articles/rose/rose.htm.

8. Josh Tyrangiel, "10 Questions for Yo-Yo Ma," *Time*, March 27, 2005, http://www.time.com/time/magazine/article/0,9171,1042474,00.html.

9. Bernard Holland, "When a Virtuoso and His Cello Take to the Road," *New York Times*, May 24, 1981.

10. Ibid.

11. Blum, *Quintet*, p. 20.

12. Carlos Prieto, *The Adventures of a Cello*, translated by Elena C. Murray (Austin, Tex.: Texas University Press, 2006), p. 24.

13. Toby Faber, *Stradivari's Genius: Five Violins, One Cello, and Three Centuries of Enduring Perfection* (New York: Random House, 2004), p. 48.

14. "Karl Davidov," http://www.cello.org/heaven/bios/davidov.htm.

15. Ibid.

16. Margaret Campbell, *The Great Cellists* (London: Victor Gallancz, 1988), p. 321.

17. Elizabeth Wilson, "Forever Young," *BBC Music Magazine* (February 2005).

18. Jessica Duchen, "Still Striking a Chord," *The Independent*, January 7, 2005.

19. Faber, *Stradivari's Genius*, p. 201.

20. Ibid.

21. Tyrangiel, "10 Questions for Yo-Yo Ma." http://www.time.com/time/magazine/article/0,9171,1042474,00.html.

22. Blum, *Quintet*, p. 35.

23. Allan Kozinn, "Young Cellists Excel in Varied Repertory," *New York Times*, January 1, 1984.

Chapter 8

MANNY, GRAMMY, AND IN THE 'HOOD WITH MR. ROGERS

The following year—1984—proved to be still more prolific in terms of recordings, with no fewer than four releases. Each was unique and revealed that there was nothing "cookie-cutter" about Yo-Yo, even relatively early in his career.

One recording was decidedly out of the mainstream. With Patricia Zander on the harpsichord, he joined the Pro Music Nipponia for a recording entitled *Yo-Yo Ma Plays Japan*. It featured selections such as "Chogoku-chino-no-kimoriuta" by Kohsaku Yamada, "Chin-chin-chidori" by Hidemaro Konoe, and "Zui-zui zukkorobashi," a traditional Japanese song. None would be familiar to Western audiences.

Another was his first crossover album, French jazz composer Claude Bolling's *Suite for Cello and Jazz Piano Trio*.

In its most basic form, crossover music is music originally written for one genre, then presented in another. In many cases, the purpose of crossover music is to appeal to a wider audience than the original version would normally command.

Perhaps the most famous classical crossover composition is the *Canon in D*, by German composer Johann Pachelbel. While Pachelbel was enormously popular and influential at the end of the seventeenth century, he and his music were mired in obscurity until the *Canon* underwent a revival in the mid-1960s. It remains instantly recognizable even today, when it is often a fixture at weddings. In dozens of variations, it has been performed and recorded by artists as diverse as the Beatles, Ozzy Osbourne, the Trans-Siberian Orchestra, and even Britney Spears.

Traditionally, classical music recordings sell just a fraction of the numbers of pop albums. With Yo-Yo's early recordings selling reasonably well, for him to begin doing crossover music was a natural progression. In general, crossover music performers have achieved success and name recognition in a particular niche and hope to build on that by appealing to a much wider audience. The Bolling recording was yet another sign that Yo-Yo was a rapidly rising star in the classical music firmament.

Claude Bolling's jazz-influenced compositions made a natural choice for a crossover album. Nearly a decade earlier, Bolling's *Suite for Flute and Jazz Piano*, featuring classical flutist Jean-Pierre Rampal, had become a smash hit. It stayed on the Billboard list of top-selling classical recordings for more than a decade, making Rampal the first crossover classical artist to achieve such a milestone.

Yo-Yo's recording of *Suite for Cello and Jazz Piano Trio* didn't enjoy the same robust sales as the Rampal album. But it would become one of the precursors for Yo-Yo's numerous future ventures outside of the strict limits of classical music.

Yo-Yo made a foray into chamber music recording for his third 1984 release when he joined forces with the Cleveland Quartet, one of the country's premier string quartets, in Franz Schubert's "Trout" Quintet. The nickname is derived from the fourth movement, a set of variations on Schubert's lied, or art song, "The Trout," originally composed for singer and piano. More formally known as the Piano Quintet in A Major, the composition departs from the usual convention of piano quintets by replacing the piano with a double bass.

Yo-Yo's recording veered away from Schubert's scoring. String quartets consist of two violins, a viola and a cello, so by adding his cello Yo-Yo in effect was taking the place of the double bass and creating a somewhat different sound.

For his fourth 1984 record, he hooked up with his good friend, pianist Emanuel Ax, in the third and fifth Beethoven sonatas for cello and piano. It was actually his second collaboration with Ax, the first one having occurred two years previously when they performed—and recorded—the first two Beethoven sonatas. These two collaborations stood as an early signpost of what has become one of the most durable and lasting collaborations in contemporary classical music. Perhaps the extraordinary kinship between Yo-Yo and Ax—whom his fellow musicians almost universally refer to as Manny—arises from correlations in their personal lives and development.

As was the case with Yo-Yo, Manny's parents were affected by World War II, though on a far deeper level. Both of them suffered the horrors of

Nazi concentration camps. They managed to survive and emerged to re-build their lives when the war ended in 1945. Manny was born four years later in Lvov, Poland, and his father became his first teacher when the boy began playing the piano at the age of six.

The Axes left Poland not long afterward and settled in Canada. Soon they moved to New York, where Manny enrolled in the Julliard precollege division. Like Yo-Yo, he chose to obtain a college education rather than beginning a concert and recording career right away. He graduated from Columbia University with a degree in French.

Manny won the inaugural Artur Rubinstein International Piano Com-petition in 1974 in Tel Aviv, Israel. From that point his career began a rapid ascent. Rubinstein, a legendary piano virtuoso, encouraged Manny and he won the Avery Fisher Prize in 1979, the year after Yo-Yo had been the recipient.

By that time their initial meeting, spurred on by mentor and famed cellist Leonard Rose in the early 1970s, had blossomed into friendship and collaboration. It helped immensely that the two young men shared the same management group, which encouraged them to do recordings together.

"I feel like I'm 20 years younger when I'm with Yo-Yo," Manny said. "By nature, pianists are a solitary lot. To tour with such a good friend is fantastic."[1]

Yo-Yo returned the favor, saying that, "Working together is all pleasure and no pitfalls."[2]

Manny adds another factor. "We're both willing to try many, many pos-sibilities and don't like to adhere to one way of doing things."[3]

Perhaps above all, as Yo-Yo told journalist Edith Eisler, "Working with Manny has meant an incredible friendship and an incredible joy, because we've been doing it for so long and known so many layers of each other that there's a shorthand of communication; we've reached the point where we can rehearse and just before the concert we can decide—let's go for this aspect, and there's enough freedom to improvise."[4]

Yo-Yo's professional success continued, but his life path was not always smooth. Late that year he had to deal with a personal tragedy. Leonard Rose died in mid-November 1984 of leukemia after a lengthy illness.

Losing him meant losing more than a friend. Rose had always believed in Yo-Yo, had mentored and encouraged him, and had helped him grow as a performer and as a person. A few years before his death, Rose wrote, "Yo-Yo has the cellistic talent and musicality of some of the greatest play-ers the world has ever known. That includes Casals, Feuermann, Rostropo-vich, and anybody else you want to name. He has a beautiful sound on the instrument, and, of course, the thing that I absolutely adore about Yo-Yo is that he is one of the nicest human beings in the world. I am proud to have been his teacher."[5]

Yo-Yo was just as proud of Rose and of his association with him. "Leonard Rose was much more than my teacher," he said. "He was my mentor and my friend. . . . He was a genuinely nice man."[6]

Rose's mentoring had affected many besides Yo-Yo. At one point in Rose's career, Rose's teacher, Felix Salmond, told him, "I predict that in time you'll become one of the greatest teachers in the world."[7] Tim Page of the *New York Times* points out a statistic confirming Salmond's prediction: "At one point, four of the cellists in the Philadelphia Orchestra, five in the New York Philharmonic, six in the Cleveland Orchestra and seven in the Boston Symphony Orchestra had been proteges of Mr. Rose. Indeed, the conductor Erich Leinsdorf used to refer to the Boston cellists as the 'Rose section.'"[8]

Though 1984 ended in sorrow for Yo-Yo because of Rose's death, the following year began in joy when he won his first Grammy award for his recording of the Bach Suites.

Much better was soon to come with the birth of his daughter Emily. Yo-Yo became even more protective of the time he had to spend with his family. In light of Emily's birth and Nicholas now becoming a toddler, it seemed especially fitting that 1985 also witnessed the first of Yo-Yo's appearances on the popular children's television show *Mister Rogers' Neighborhood*.

During this appearance and in a number of subsequent visits, host Fred Rogers didn't showcase Yo-Yo as a guest star. Instead, he used Yo-Yo to help inspire his viewers. For example, Rogers might try to play the cello himself—rather badly, it turned out. Then he would turn to Yo-Yo and ask him to play a little. Yo-Yo would comply. Even to very young and very untrained ears, the contrast would be obvious. Did you always play this well, Rogers would then ask. Yo-Yo, of course, shook his head. How did you get to be this good, Rogers would pursue. By practicing, Yo-Yo said. A lot of practicing.

So in his gentle, low-key manner, Rogers made sure that his viewers got the point without talking down to them or preaching. No practice = squeaks and squawks. Lots of practice = beautiful music. It did require hard work, but success was in their own hands. If kids also began to develop an appreciation for classical music, that was even better.

There is plenty of evidence that kids who watched Mister Rogers' Neighborhood when Yo-Yo appeared did develop an appreciation for classical music. And some viewers went well beyond simply developing an appreciation. Rogers cited one example: "We heard about a four-year-old in Chicago who heard Yo Yo Ma for the first time on our program. He pointed to the television set and said, 'I do that.' His parents thought that was sweet but he said it again the next day and finally badgered them so that they found a Suzuki class and started him with a one sixteenth size cello. That kid is now in college and still playing the cello. His mother, who had to help with practice, got interested in the cello and is now part of a string quartet in their town."[9]

That little boy and his mother certainly weren't the only ones to catch the classical music bug from seeing Yo-Yo play for Mr. Rogers. Cellist Clark Pang, who made his Carnegie Hall debut in 2007 at the age of 10, also got his start from watching the show. In this case, he was inspired when Yo-Yo used his cello to mimic the sound of a fire engine.

A third example was Esperanza Spalding, who was inspired to begin playing the violin at the age of four when she watched Yo-Yo on the show. She continued violin lessons for 11 years before being introduced to the bass. As had been the case with Yo-Yo and the cello, it was love at first sight. She quickly developed an affinity for jazz and released her first album, *Junjo,* in 2006 to excellent reviews. She is now a jazz instructor and sought-after performer.

Mr. Rogers' Neighborhood wasn't the only kids' show on which Yo-Yo appeared. He was also a guest on *Sesame Street* on several occasions. For one episode he played the lead part in the "Beethoven Quartet for Two Honkers, Dinger and Cello." Murray Beethoven, that is—a muppet who was one of the other three members of the impromptu group. Characteristically, Yo-Yo easily interacted with his fellow "players," finishing with a grand flourish and shaking their hands as the audience applauded.

Somewhat tongue in cheek, he discussed another Sesame Street appearance. "I knew Elmo [one of the show's major characters] before he became a superstar and while he was learning the violin. He was not too good at it. He was playing a scale and *na-na-na-na-neh.* He couldn't quite get to that last note. I helped him through his problem."[10]

In 1999, Yo-Yo became a giant bunny with floppy ears on the popular PBS animated show *Arthur.* One of the characters wanted him to play his cello for a concert.

Yo-Yo relished these and other opportunities to reach out to children and has said that they are among the things he's proudest of. One reason is that he identifies with children. "I've always had mischief in my soul,"[11] he happily confesses. On a more serious level, he adds, "So often, music education seems to be about bringing kids to the concert hall, which is great, but on the TV show I was a guest invited into their world. That's really powerful, and it means that the cello and a cellist is never going to be an unfamiliar figure to those kids."[12]

Yo-Yo hasn't confined his influence on young people to television appearances. While his busy schedule keeps him from teaching on a regular basis, he makes time as often as he can for opportunities to work closely with students, especially in master classes. Master classes are intense sessions for advanced musicians, taught by someone who has achieved particular distinction with his or instrument.

Fred Rogers vividly remembered being able to sit in on one of those master classes, which Yo-Yo conducted for several cellists in the Pittsburgh Youth Symphony. Terming him "the most other-oriented genius I've ever known," Rogers continued, "Yo-Yo gently led those young cellists into understandings about their instruments, their music, and their selves, which some of them told me later, they'd carry with them forever."[13]

Yo-Yo also makes a point of reaching out to youngsters during his regular concert appearances. Roger Chang, an amateur cellist, has vivid memories of one such occasion when Yo-Yo welcomed a throng of eager young fans into his dressing room after a performance. He posed for photos and signed autographs. "What he has done to make classical music popular alone surpasses what dozens of other musicians combined have done,"[14] Chang says.

Yet another effort in this direction came in 1987 with the release of *King Midas and the Golden Touch*. The half-hour videotape was one of a series of films by Rabbit Ears Productions, in which noted actors—in this case, Michael Caine—read famous legends and fairy tales that had been adapted for youngsters. Yo-Yo played the musical background along with jazz pianist Ellis Marsalis, who also composed it.

Official recognition of all his efforts came on the south lawn of the White House in October, 1994, when President Bill Clinton presented 11 distinguished American artists with the National Medal of the Arts. The august group included singers Harry Belafonte and Pete Seeger, and actor/dancer Gene Kelly.

Clinton also awarded a medal to Young Audiences Incorporated. He said that the organization "has been instrumental in bringing the enrichment of performing arts to millions of young people all across our country. That is a terrific achievement, and I am honored to present the medal to one of our most outstanding young musicians, Yo Yo Ma."[15]

While it may have been a stretch to call Yo-Yo a "young musician" (he had celebrated his 39th birthday several days before the ceremony), it was particularly significant that Clinton chose to present Yo-Yo with the award on behalf of Young Audiences Incorporated. It marked public recognition at the highest level of his unflagging efforts to make classical music more accessible to young people.

But there is one arena of musical function into which he refuses to step. On one occasion, he served on the jury during a formal cello competition. The experience was so distasteful that he vowed never to do it again. "Every time someone invites me, I say, 'I'm sorry, I will do anything you want with the winners or with the losers, but I will not be a judge," he said.[16]

Yo-Yo's obvious talent from an early age contrasts with his own less-than-stellar history in competitions. "I lost every competition I ever tried—no, that's not true; I won a competition when I was five years old," he said "That was the highlight of my career."[17] He was turned down three times in auditions for Leonard Bernstein's Young People's Concerts, and finished out of the running in the Gregory Piatigorsky Competition (named for the Russian-born cellist who became very prominent during the middle third of the twentieth century) while he was at Harvard.

His competition experiences notwithstanding, Yo-Yo's objections to competition go far deeper than a simple case of sour grapes. He explains that judging among individuals who may be very different in temperament, style and relative strengths and weaknesses is, in essence, comparing apples and oranges and deciding that one is "better" than the other. He further objects to the necessity of breaking down auditions into various categories with assigned point values, thereby destroying the integrity of a young musician's overall performance. A third issue—and given his feelings about the value of a broad education perhaps the most telling—is the deleterious effect of the pressures of being a competition winner and the attendant push toward immediate performance.

"I believe that the years between 15 and 20-something are the most essential to your development; everything you learn during that time is there for you to draw upon for the rest of your life," Yo-Yo says. "If you put a lot into producing concerts instead of trying to open yourself to learning different ways of making music, you'll be a diminished person"[18]—and a diminished musician. Youth is a time for experimentation, he strongly believes. Musicians unwilling to experiment when they are young aren't likely to change their ways as they grow older. They fall into predictable patterns and cease growing artistically.

An opportunity to expand his views on competition—and have them validated by a respected figure—came in March of 1986 in a program officially billed as the 10th anniversary of the establishment of the Avery Fisher Artist Program. The animating spirit of the concert was the celebration of Fisher's 80th birthday.

All seven recipients of the Avery Fisher Prize were on hand. Shortly before the performance, Fisher reflected on the nature of the prize in words with which Yo-Yo almost certainly would have agreed. "This [the awarding of the prize] should not be a competition," Fisher said. "I consider it an affront to have a human being appear on a platform, knowing that there's a jury out in the darkened auditorium, and that the next half hour may be the turning point of his life. That's no way to treat a sensitive performing person. I feel that competitions are barbaric."[19]

Manny Ax agreed with Fisher, explaining that in general he too didn't believe in awards. "But the Avery Fisher Prize is a special kind of recognition, and what makes it so tremendously gratifying is that it comes from your peers, who recommend you for it," he said. "It's more like the Pulitzer or Nobel Prizes, in that it acknowledges that you've achieved something worthwhile."[20]

Before taking the stage, Yo-Yo added, "I think it [the Avery Fisher Prize] conveys a sense of psychological well-being. It tells you that people you respect believe in you and support what you're doing. And I guess that's what makes a career, if you want to look at it that way."[21]

Both Yo-Yo and Manny had received a boost to their respective careers a few weeks earlier at the Grammy Awards, when they won for their recording of Johannes Brahms' Sonatas No. 1 and No. 2 for Cello and Piano. Yo-Yo also scored a Grammy in Classical Performance—Instrumental Soloist with Orchestra for his recording of the Elgar and Walton Cello Concertos with André Previn and the London Symphony Orchestra.

More than any other work, the Elgar concerto is associated with Jacqueline du Pré. On numerous occasions, Yo-Yo has said that he feels a great deal of emotion every time he plays it. Not only is there poignancy in the memory of du Pré's tragic loss of her career to multiple sclerosis, but Yo-Yo's own dynamic upward ascent encountered something of a roadblock in 1987 when du Pré passed away.

Her Davidov cello was put up for sale and Yo-Yo was given the first chance to buy it, at a price considerably below market value. Even at that reduced level, he would have had to add substantially to his already grueling concert schedule to pay for it, perhaps for as long as 10 years. His daughter Emily had been added to his family, and he wanted to be with Jill, Nicholas, and Emily as much as possible. Spending even more time away from home to pay for another instrument was an unacceptable burden. He declined. The Davidov went back to Vatelot.

The matter might have ended there, and the Davidov would have wound up with someone else—most likely in a private collection. But in the close-knit classical music world a wealthy patron heard about the situation. This patron (who remains anonymous) purchased the cello and returned it to Yo-Yo with an especially generous proviso—he would be able to use it for the rest of his performing career.

It goes without saying that Yo-Yo is particularly careful with his priceless instruments. During his frequent travels, his cellos travel with him, and always in first class. The expense of purchasing an extra ticket for his cello is more than compensated for by the peace of mind that comes from having it close at hand. Putting his instruments in the cargo hold, even if heavily padded, would be an invitation to disaster.

On one occasion, this manner of transporting his cellos nearly prevented him from catching a flight to a concert. When he arrived at the airline check-in counter, there was no trace of any reservation for his Davidov cello. Every seat on the plane was occupied, so the harried ticket counter person told Yo-Yo that the only place for it was in the hold. Yo-Yo refused, and a standoff ensued. With the time until takeoff running increasingly short, Yo-Yo insisted on seeing the passenger list. When he perused the list, he found what he was looking for. There was indeed a seat for the Davidov. It had been listed under the name "Mr. Cabinba"—airline shorthand for cabin baggage.

On one famous occasion he wasn't careful enough. In October of 1999, he had a strenuous evening performance. The next afternoon, he got into a taxi. He put "Petunia," his Montagnana cello—which carried a valuation of about two and a half million dollars—in its protective plastic case into the trunk of the cab. About 20 minutes later, he arrived at the hotel where he was staying, paid the driver, and walked inside. The cab sped away—with Petunia still in the trunk.

A few minutes later, he realized what had happened. Fortunately, he still had the receipt from his ride, which contained the taxi's medallion number. That set off a massive cello hunt. Police cars received an all-points bulletin, alerting them to keep an eye out for the cab. Another frantic call went to the office of Mayor Rudy Giuliani, where staffers contacted the city's Taxi and Limousine Commission. In turn, the commission dispatched some of its inspectors to join the search. The situation was especially fraught with pressure. The cab could be rear-ended in traffic, seriously damaging the cello. Someone might steal it. And Yo-Yo had a concert early that evening. Without his cello, he would have to cancel it.

Somehow the cab managed to elude the hundreds of official vehicles looking for it. One reason was that most of them were looking in the wrong place. The taxi's home base was in Queens, on Long Island, several miles away from the borough of Manhattan where Yo-Yo had gotten into and out of the cab. Fortunately, a patrol car from Queens had been

dispatched to the cab's home base. It arrived just as the driver was com-
pleting his shift.

By that time, the media had become aware of the search. Newspaper
reporters and television news crews converged on the hotel. That in turn
attracted hundreds of passersby, who joined Ma in his anxious vigil.

Soon they got the good news. Police officers had popped the cab's trunk
and found the cello, still in its plastic case and undamaged. A short time
later it was back in Yo-Yo's hands.

"I did something really stupid," Yo-Yo told reporters. "I was in such a
rush, I was so exhausted, I'd given a concert at Carnegie Hall last night. I
just forgot. Somehow magic happened, and I have my cello. The instrument is my voice. So I need it."[22]

The bizarre incident capped one of the most remarkable periods in the
career of any performer in any artistic genre. As one writer noted a short
time later, "During the last decade or so Ma has leaped off into multiple
new trajectories, exploring diverse worlds of folk, crossover music, and
multimedia experimentation."[23]

Yo-Yo's varied achievements during that decade marked the full fruition of the process that had begun when he made the fateful decision
to attend Harvard rather than rushing into a performing career. He did
indeed need his cello.

NOTES

1. Tim Page, "Ma and Ax: A Special Blend of Cello and Piano," *New York
Times*, November 16, 1984.

2. Ibid.

3. Andrew L. Pincus, *Musicians with a Mission: Keeping the Classical Tradition
Alive* (Boston: Northeastern University Press, 2002), p. 16.

4. Edith Eisler, "Yo-Yo Ma: Music from the Soul," *Strings* (May/June 1992),
p. 49.

5. Tim Janof, "Leonard Rose Remembered," http://www.cello.org/Newsletter/
Articles/rose/rose.htm.

6. Tim Page, "Leonard Rose Benefit," *New York Times*, November 1, 1986.

7. Janof, "Leonard Rose Remembered."

8. Page, "Leonard Rose Benefit."

9. "Mr. Rogers' Passion for Learning," http://www.aarp.org/nrta/Articles/
a2002–12–19-nrta_rogers.html.

10. Pincus, *Musicians with a Mission*, pp. 7–8.

11. Gerri Hirshey, "We Are the World (Cellist Yo-Yo Ma)," *Parade*, January 30, 2005.

12. Paul Cutts, "Caravans in the Desert," *The Guardian*, September 7, 2007.

13. "Fred McFeely Rogers: 2002 Commencement Address at Dartmouth College," http://www.indigo.org/mrrogers.html.

14. Pincus, *Musicians with a Mission*, p. 7.

15. President Bill Clinton, "Remarks on Presenting Arts and Humanities Awards," http://www.encyclopedia.com/doc/1G1–16424016.html.

16. Eisler, "Yo-Yo Ma: Music from the Soul," p. 53.

17. Ibid.

18. Ibid, p. 54.

19. Allan Kozinn, "A Benefactor Tells Why He Did It," *New York Times*, March 2, 1986.

20. Ibid.

21. Ibid.

22. Beth Gardiner, "Yo-Yo Ma Forgets Cello in Cab, but Cops Get It Back," *South Coast Today*, October 17, 1999.

23. Janet Tassel, "Yo-Yo Ma's Journeys," *Harvard Magazine*, March–April 2000.

Chapter 9

A JAZZ LEGEND AND FAREWELL TO A FATHER

No one—least of all Yo-Yo—would maintain that his career took a radical turn at the beginning of this period. Rather, it was more a case of his willingness to experiment. He was starting to move into musical overdrive. He could afford to stretch beyond conventional expectations regarding a classical musician of his stature. He had already established a solid foundation of musical sensitivity and depth through his concert appearances, 10 years' worth of recordings, four Grammys, and community work such as teaching and appearing on children's shows.

This solid foundation was evidenced by the release in 1989 of his album, *A Portrait of Yo-Yo Ma*. Apart from "The Swan" from Saint-Saëns' *Carnival of the Animals*, everything on *Portrait* had been previously recorded. It was therefore in essence his first "Greatest Hits" album.

Nineteen eighty-nine, which would become Yo-Yo's most prolific recording year up to that point, continued with four albums of twentieth-century music. These four albums included major works by well-known composers Samuel Barber, Benjamin Britten, and Dmitri Shostakovich—musically speaking, the relatively conventional—and it also contained the relatively exotic: *Rejoice, for Violin and Cello*, by Sofia Gubaidulina, a Russian composer of Tatar ancestry. His recording of Barber's Cello Concerto and Britten's Symphony for Cello and Orchestra, with David Zinman conducting the Baltimore Symphony Orchestra, earned him a Grammy.

He made another Japanese album, a combination of selections from his 1984 recording and new material. A number of artists were included in this undertaking, among them Jean-Pierre Rampal, the classical flutist whose album of Claude Bolling's *Suite for Flute and Jazz Piano* had been a smash crossover hit during the 1970s.

Also in 1989, Yo-Yo made another foray into jazz, working with famed French jazz violinist Stéphane Grappelli.

Like Yo-Yo, Grappelli owed his introduction to music to his father; his early life was otherwise dissimilar to Yo-Yo's. Grappelli was born in 1908. He lost his mother to disease when he was just four. The outbreak of World War I in 1914 compounded the young Grappelli's difficulties. His father was called into military service and the boy spent the war years in an orphanage.

He and his father were reunited when the war ended in 1918. They lived in poverty. Shortly afterward, his father bought him a violin. Grappelli proved to be a natural talent and soon became a busker, a person who plays in the streets and depends on the goodwill of passersby to generate even a modest income. At the age of 15 he obtained regular work, playing the piano to accompany silent films.

"In the cinema, I had to play Mozart principally but was allowed some Gershwin in funny films. Then I discovered jazz and my vocation and kissed Amadeus goodbye,"[1] he later said.

It was perhaps the longest "kiss" in musical history. Grappelli's "vocation" lasted for nearly 80 years, for he remained a vigorous and critically acclaimed performer virtually up to his death in 1997. He was 81 when he and Yo-Yo recorded their jazz album. Several years later, on the occasion of his 85th birthday, someone asked if he was considering retirement. Grappelli replied: "Retirement! There isn't a word that is more painful to my ears. Music keeps me going. It has given me everything. It's my fountain of youth."[2]

Yo-Yo of course is still many years shy of Grappelli's age level, but no one would be surprised to hear him expressing a similar sentiment—though in all likelihood he would not attribute his ongoing youthfulness to music alone but would also include his family. "At the end of life, you never regret not having done another project, but you always regret if you have not spent enough time with loved ones,"[3] he said during an interview.

Yo-Yo and Grappelli will almost certainly share another similarity at some point in the future. A few months before his death, Grappelli joined the music industry's most prominent heavyweights when he received the Grammy Lifetime Achievement Award. Yo-Yo's good friend and multi-Grammy winner, violinist Itzhak Perlman, enjoyed a similar nod in 2008. It seems only a matter of time until Yo-Yo is so honored.

The result of the 1989 collaboration between Grappelli and Yo-Yo was an album called *Anything Goes*. It was largely based on Cole Porter tunes.

Porter was one of the most prolific American songwriters in the first half of the twentieth century, with more than two dozen Broadway hits and hundreds of individual songs to his credit.

Yo-Yo had been part of Grappelli's 80th birthday celebration the previous year, at Carnegie Hall. "The cellist Yo Yo Ma gave a premier performance to a pleasant three-movement jazz chamber piece, 'Two Moods of Blues,' composed for the occasion by the pianist Roger Kellaway," wrote critic Stephen Holden. "In performing it, the cellist took bold tonal liberties, bending notes flat to underscore the melodies' blues orientation and boldly alternating between a rich lustrous timbre and a harsher, more abrasive sound."[4]

The critical mood was considerably different the following year when they gave another live performance, timing it to coincide with the release of *Anything Goes*. After praising Grappelli's violin work, Peter Watrous of the *New York Times* complained that "Grappelli also played with a flat-footed group, including the cellist Yo-Yo Ma, put together by Roger Kellaway; the group had the jazz sensibility of a brick wall and the marketing sensibility of Madison Avenue. It buried Mr. Grappelli's personality, which probably wasn't the point."[5]

In addition to the criticism of Yo-Yo's personal performance, the album itself received a somewhat mixed reception. On the supportive side, Ken Dryden of *All Music Guide* noted, "The cellist seems to be gradually getting his feet wet on the opening title track, but becomes more prominent on 'Easy to Love' and cuts loose on 'I Concentrate On You.'. . . Overall, it's a fun session worth picking up."[6]

On the less supportive side, Ed Siegel of the *Boston Globe* commented that Yo-Yo's "one attempt at jazz (sic), 'Anything Goes' with Stephane Grappelli, was not a success because anything didn't. The fault seemed to lie less with Ma than with the antiseptic production and arrangement. . . . The producers would have been better off getting out of the way and just letting Grappelli and Ma go at it."[7]

It didn't take long for Yo-Yo to "go at it" in another direction. While one reason for these various ventures into new areas was doubtless Yo-Yo's wide-ranging intellectual and musical curiosity, another reason was more practical: The cello literature is relatively limited. For example, Mozart's vast symphonic output included 27 piano concertos and 5 violin concertos. Beethoven wrote 5 piano concertos and a single violin concerto. Neither wrote any symphonic music specifically for the cello, though Beethoven did include a cello as a solo instrument in the Triple Concerto.

As Manny Ax once explained, "A pianist could go on playing for 100 years and not begin to play the complete standard repertoire. For a cellist, if you are a talent like Yo-Yo, by the time you are 25 you have mastered all the cello concertos that are known."[8]

Taking note of the paucity of cello works by the biggest names in the classical canon, Rostropovich said, "The piano has an enormous repertoire. The violin, less, but still quite enough. The cello? It is like we are unemployed. . . . If I had been there when Beethoven was alive, I would have terrorized him until he wrote at least three concertos for the cello."[9]

Rostropovich pioneered one way of enlarging the cello repertoire. Through commissions and other means, Rostropovich is credited with adding more than 200 works to the cello repertoire.

"Of all the incredible things Slava [Rostropovich's nickname] has done in his life, and the list is huge, this will be his greatest, most enduring legacy," Yo-Yo said.[10] But Yo-Yo has done a very similar thing, with results similar to Rostropovich's.

"No other American cellist—and probably no single American musician—has been responsible for the birthing of so many works in so many genres and idioms," notes Andrew L. Pincus. "Together, Ma and Rostropovich have greatly expanded the solo cello literature, at the same time giving many composers support and exposure."[11]

One of the first commissions for Yo-Yo was Stephen Albert's Cello Concerto, which he premiered in May, 1990, with the Baltimore Symphony. It received a rapturous critical reception.

According to USA Today, "Ma unveiled something of unusual significance, Stephen Albert's entrancing Cello Concerto. . . . When you give yourself over to the emotional state it attempts to create, it hits you in the solar plexus. What a wonderfully protracted discovery it's going to be for performers and audiences."[12]

Another new work associated with Yo-Yo from this time was among the most unusual compositions he ever played: Begin Again Again, . . . by American composer Tod Machover.

Machover was a classically trained cellist who graduated from Juilliard. He was also very interested in rock music—both as performer and as listener—and in technology, particularly computers. He wanted to combine these interests, so he began developing what he called "hyperinstruments" at the Massachusetts Institute of Technology in the mid-1980s. These instruments allowed musicians to produce increasingly complex sounds by routing them through computers, which augmented and altered them and played them back through a system of loudspeakers. The procedure allowed a handful of musicians and technicians to replicate the sound of a much larger ensemble.

Machover began working with Yo-Yo in 1990, and wrote *Begin Again Again . . .* with him in mind. He also designed a "hypercello" for Yo-Yo to play. It resembled a cello in its basic shape, but was considerably flatter, somewhat like an electric guitar.

While he was playing the hypercello, Yo-Yo wore an electronic bracelet on his right wrist, which sent signals to several Mac II computers controlled by Machover and several of his colleagues. Combined with several other wires and sensors, the result was the production of data on several factors such as bow pressure and the way that he fingered the strings with his left hand. Machover and the others manipulated the input through their computers to transform Yo-Yo's original sound.

Begin Again Again . . . was based on the sarabande of Bach's Suite No. 2 for Solo Cello, with which Machover was familiar because of his cello background. According to Machover, the composition "serves as a metaphor for change in our lives—of breaking with the past while retaining what is dearest to us; of opening up doors to unknown possibilities; and finally, of renewed hope and affirmation."[13]

The composition received its premiere in the summer of 1991 at the Tanglewood Festival. Founded in 1940 in the Berkshire Mountains in Western Massachusetts, Tanglewood is the summer home of the Boston Symphony Orchestra. It also incorporates many other performances and is one of the most prestigious musical events in the country.

Machover's title referred to the structure of the composition. It had 10 separate sections, which were grouped into two larger movements. It was based on several variations of melody and harmony, which Yo-Yo continually returned to, though with each repetition the material was altered and expanded.

"The music sauntered and screamed," said critic Edward Rothstein. "The speakers echoed Mr. Ma and anticipated him, fragmenting his sound and recombining its elements. Again and again, the cello and its electronic ghost would drive the pitch upward, sometimes painfully, and then break its drive, cascading into lyricism."[14]

Rothstein may have heard "lyricism." It's likely that other listeners simply heard noise. Respected music journalist Edith Eisler perhaps expressed the viewpoint of many when she said, "I found the project thoroughly baffling from a mechanical point of view and hard to react to as a piece of music."[15]

Yo-Yo didn't neglect performing his customary classical repertoire either, though at times he gave even that a unique twist. For example, earlier that year he played all six Bach cello suites in a single marathon performance at Carnegie Hall. He played three of the suites—the equivalent of a full recital—after which he took an hour's break, then returned to play the other three.

"Presenting Bach's Six Solo Suites for Cello in one long gulp is an adventure in concentration for both listener and performer," commented reviewer Bernard Holland. "Through subtle variations of pressure, every layer of harmony, either real or implied, danced lightly into the ear."[16]

That particular concert had an unusual postscript. A celebration following the performance lasted until well after midnight. When it was over, Yo-Yo returned to the apartment where his in-laws lived, looking forward to a long and restful sleep. Unfortunately, he found himself without a key. He banged on the apartment door but couldn't wake up anyone. Finally he lay down on the hallway floor outside the door, laid his head on his overcoat, and tried to get some rest.

He encountered smoother sailing later that year when he received an honorary doctorate from Harvard. Its award just 15 years after he had received his bachelor's degree reflected the high esteem in which his alma mater held him. Now, like his father, he was Dr. Ma.

The timing proved to be poignant. His father, Hiao-Tsiun, died just a few months later, on August 28. One of Hiao-Tsiun's last memories was of Yo-Yo playing the sarabande from the fifth Bach cello suite at his bedside. It was part of the music that he had given Yo-Yo to practice so many years before. Now it became part of the final chapter in his own life. In a sense, listening to his son play for him brought his life full circle and confirmed his long-held belief that good musicians come from the third generation of a family.

His son's success wasn't Hiao-Tsiun's only satisfaction. He had been closely associated with the Children's Orchestra until he retired in 1977 and moved to Taiwan. In 1984, Yeou-Cheng—who by that time had become a successful physician—and her husband, Michael Dadap, revived it. Today the orchestra involves hundreds of young musicians and remains a fixture in the New York cultural scene. And even though Hiao-Tsiun's original Carnegie Hall aspirations had only involved his son, he would undoubtedly have been proud that his daughter also made it to the venue's august precinct in 2007 when the Children's Orchestra made its first appearance there.

Hiao-Tsiun must have been amazed at how successful his son had become. As he had dreamt more than three decades earlier, the name "Yo-Yo Ma" had indeed been emblazoned prominently on the marquee of Carnegie Hall—as well as on many of the world's other major concert venues.

And Yo-Yo Ma was just getting warmed up.

NOTES

1. Lee Yanowitch, "French Jazz Violinist Stephane Grappelli Dead At 89," http://www.cyberbites.com/marleys_ghost/grappelliobit.html.

2. Ibid.

3. Mabel Jong, "Yo-Yo Ma: Family Is Best Investment," http://www.bankrate.com/brm/news/investing/20030821a1.asp.

4. Stephen Holden, "Grappelli, 80, Stars at His Tribute," *New York Times*, April 16, 1988.

5. Peter Watrous, "Grappelli at Carnegie Hall, Still Seeking New Options," *New York Times*, October 8, 1989.

6. Ken Dryden, "phane Grappelli—Discography: Anything Goes, with Yo Yo Ma," *All Music Guide*, http://www.legacyrecordings.com/Stephane-Grappelli-with-Yo-Yo-Ma/Anything-Goes-The-Music-of-Cole-Porter.aspx.

7. Ed Siegel, "Playing the Full Human Range: Yo-Yo Ma Plays the Cello to Create a Portrait of the Artist," *Boston Globe*, August 6, 1995.

8. Bruce Handy and Daniel S. Levy, "Yo-Yo Ma's Suite Life?" *Time*, March 23, 1998.

9. Anthony Tommasini, "A Cellist Continually in Search of an Author," *New York Times*, March 26, 1995.

10. Ibid.

11. Andrew L. Pincus, *Musicians with a Mission: Keeping the Classical Tradition Alive* (Boston: Northeastern University Press, 2002), p. 24.

12. "Stephen Albert—Cello Concerto," http://209.218.170.3/composers/albert_cello_concerto.html.

13. "Begin Again Again," http://web.media.mit.edu/~tod/Tod/begin.html.

14. Edward Rothstein, "Review/Music; Yo-Yo Ma and His New 'Hyper' Cello," *New York Times*, August 17, 1991.

15. Edith Eisler, "Yo-Yo Ma: Music from the Soul," *Strings* (May/June) 1992, pp. 48–49.

16. Bernard Holland, "Review/Cello: Yo-Yo Ma Personalizes Six Bach Suites," *New York Times*, January 15, 1991.

Yo-Yo Ma appearing on the long-running PBS television program Mister Rogers' Neighborhood. *Yo-Yo visited* Mister Rogers' Neighborhood *several times, beginning in the mid-1980s. Here, Fred Rogers, with Yo-Yo's encouragement, attempts to play the cello. (Courtesy of Photofest)*

Undated photograph of Pablo Casals directing a chamber ensemble. The legendary Casals rediscovered Bach's suites for unaccompanied cello, revolutionizing the music world's view of Bach. In 1962 Casals introduced Yo-Yo Ma to Leonard Bernstein, who featured Yo-Yo and Yeou-Cheng, along with Casals and others, in a televised benefit concert for a national performing arts center. (New York World-Telegram and the Sun Newspaper Photograph Collection/Courtesy of the Library of Congress/LC-USZ62-118257)

Renowned cellist Mstislav Rostropovich and his wife, the Bolshoi Opera soprano Galina Vishnevskaya, in 1965. Yo-Yo followed Rostropovich in commissioning many new compositions to expand the cello repertoire. (Stanley Wolfson/New York World-Telegram and the Sun Newspaper Photograph Collection/Courtesy of the Library of Congress/LC-USZ62-115062)

Yo-Yo and longtime friend and musical partner Emanuel Ax perform under a portrait of philanthropist Avery Fisher at a benefit concert in Fisher's honor held at Avery Fisher Hall in New York City, May 1994. (AP Images/ Bebeto Matthews)

Yo-Yo, dancer Tina Fehlandt, and choreographer Mark Morris rehearse Morris's dance The Argument at the Wang Center in Boston, February 1999. Yo-Yo and Morris also collaborated on Falling Down Stairs, one of the Inspired by Bach films. (AP Images/Elise Amendola)

Yo-Yo Ma communicates his enthusiasm and love of music during a lively master class workshop held in Taipei in May 2000. (AP Images/Wally Santana)

Yo-Yo performs with the Silk Road Ensemble at Carnegie Hall in New York City, May 2002. The musician in the center plays a horse-head fiddle. (AP Images/Osamu Honda)

Yo-Yo and his wife, Jill Hornor, were among the guests at a November 2005 White House dinner honoring Britain's Prince Charles and his wife, Camilla, Duchess of Cornwall. (AP Images/Haraz N. Ghanbari)

Chapter 10

HUSH AND HAPPINESS
IN SMALL GROUPS

Yo-Yo's penchant for apparently offbeat pairings continued with his 1992 album *Hush*, in conjunction with Bobby McFerrin.

At first glance, McFerrin would have seemed an unlikely collaborator for Yo-Yo. He had become famous in 1988 when his pop single, "Don't Worry, Be Happy," was a chart-topper and won the Grammy for Best Song the following year. The thing that especially set McFerrin apart was the phenomenal range of his voice—which spanned four octaves—and his uncanny ability to use it to mimic the sound of musical instruments. On one memorable occasion, he simultaneously replicated a bass and a drum, using his voice as the string instrument while creating drumbeats by pounding on his chest. He also enjoyed a strong reputation as a jazz musician.

Despite the direction that his career had taken, McFerrin actually came from a classical music background. Robert McFerrin, Sr., his father, had the distinction of being the first African-American male singer to appear with the Metropolitan Opera, and his mother was a singer and vocal instructor. McFerrin joked that while he was growing up, one of his favorite hiding places was under the piano that occupied a prominent place in the family home.

Yo-Yo met McFerrin at the Tanglewood Festival in 1988 on the occasion of Leonard Bernstein's 70th birthday party. Both had been aware of—and admiring of—each other for some time before that. Their first collaboration came in 1990. McFerrin had decided that he wanted not only to perform music, but also to conduct it. He threw himself completely into the project of becoming a conductor, buttonholing anyone he could find who could help him and also reading voluminously on the subject. His debut came on his 40th birthday, when he conducted the San Francisco Orchestra as it played Beethoven's Seventh Symphony. The work had special meaning for him. It had been the first symphony he heard, at the age of 12, and his sister had been part of the violin section.

McFerrin invited Yo-Yo to be part of the evening, and told him that the two of them would do a series of improvisations. Yo-Yo wasn't comfortable with that, and asked McFerrin to write out something for him to play. Finally McFerrin did—and then changed it just before the concert.

Despite Yo-Yo's uneasiness, the concert proved to be enjoyable. "He [McFerrin] can lead you into doing something without your knowing you can do it," he said. "The idea is just to go with it. Bobby's personality allowed me to be in that frame of mind, to do whatever I felt like doing without feeling that I was being judged in some way."[1]

After intermission McFerrin conducted the Beethoven. Sharp-eyed concertgoers such as writer Joshua Koshman may have noticed an extra person in the orchestra: "There was Ma, sitting in the back row of the orchestra's cello section, playing along and grinning like a kid who'd just slipped past the guards at the ballpark and positioned himself behind third base. By any reckoning, he should have been relaxing in his dressing room or heading back to the hotel. But there was music going on, and he couldn't stay away."[2]

Yo-Yo and McFerrin collaborated again early the following year, in a benefit for the Boston Philharmonic Orchestra. Once again Yo-Yo sat unobtrusively in the rear of the cello section as McFerrin conducted part of Beethoven's Eighth Symphony. Then they joined forces to do what they do best: Yo-Yo playing the cello and McFerrin mimicking the sounds of various other instruments. Critic Richard Dyer captured the spirit of the evening in noting that, "McFerrin led the orchestra, audience, and solo cellist in an improvised 'Concerto' that was so much fun one wondered why we shouldn't just dispense with our political leaders and substitute McFerrin; he could lead the nations in singing and creating, which makes more sense than raging furiously together."[3]

When *Hush* was released in 1992, it contained much of the same material that McFerrin and Ma had performed live. The *Boston Globe's* Ed Siegel was just as unimpressed with the album as he had been with *Anything Goes*. While noting that *Hush* sold well, he harrumphed, "I have to admit that McFerrin's body-thumping and wide-ranging vocal charms elude me. They seem emblematic of a too-cute strain in the classical-music world that no one in the field, Ma included, is immune to."[4]

Siegel wasn't the only critic to pan *Hush*. Linda Sanders of *Entertainment Weekly* gave it a D+ rating. While conceding that it had "moments of real artistry amid long stretches of annoying jive," she complained that "[It] is actively painful, consisting mainly of voice- and-cello versions of stale classics (even 'Flight of the Bumblebee,' for cripe's sakes), all supposedly made intriguing because McFerrin sings what's usually played (far better) on an instrument."[5]

Not surprisingly, Dyer, Siegel's *Boston Globe* colleague, felt differently. While noting that the recording didn't have the same spontaneity or interchange between the two men of their live performances, he added that it was "a quiet, unpretentious album of mostly unimportant music that gives pleasure because of the pleasure the performers take in making it. . . . The performances and musicianship are on a very high level, and you can tell that Yo-Yo Ma and Bobby McFerrin made this record because they liked each other and wanted to. It wasn't some high-powered executive sitting around in an office who thought this one up."[6]

The album's cover expresses this spirit. It shows a smiling McFerrin with his arm around Yo-Yo, whose smile is equal in intensity. Both men are casually attired in sweatshirts and are obviously enjoying each other's company.

The record-buying public turned out to be solidly on Dyer's side. *Hush* stayed on the Billboard crossover chart for months and continues to sell briskly today, well over 20 years after its release.

On a more serious level, Yo-Yo released six other albums in 1992, of which two became Grammy winners. One of these two contained classical music pieces for cello and orchestra written by the Russian composers Sergei Prokofiev and Peter Tchaikovsky, and played by the Pittsburgh Symphony Orchestra, with Lorin Maazel conducting. The other winning album, made with Manny Ax, consisted of three Brahms sonatas for cello and piano. Yo-Yo and Ax had been part of a winning team before: the previous year, they had joined forces with violinist Isaac Stern and violist Jaime Laredo for still another Grammy winner, two Brahms piano quartets.

The two chamber music Grammys marked a shift in the direction of Yo-Yo's recording career. Although his first decade had included some chamber music albums (two of which won Grammys), its primary thrust was in the direction of big-name compositions such as the Dvořák, Schumann, and Haydn concertos. In two successive years—1987 and 1988—he had recorded different versions of Johannes Brahms's Double Concerto in A Minor with the Chicago Symphony Orchestra. The first was with Itzhak Perlman and conductor Daniel Barenboim, while the second, under the baton of Claudio Abbado, matched Yo-Yo and Isaac Stern as the soloists. This emphasis on well-known orchestral pieces was an entirely reasonable path for a musician seeking to establish himself.

By now, of course, Yo-Yo was fully established as a renowned classical musician. The 1992 Prokofiev/Tchaikovsky recording was his only effort with a full orchestra since his similar Grammy-winner—the Britten and Barber concertos—in 1989. He had the freedom to play and record more of the chamber music he so enjoyed.

Yo-Yo has traced his love of chamber music back to his early teens. This affection is associated in particular with his first summer away from home at Meadowmount in 1971, when he was 15. In much the same way that youngsters today might get together to play video games or a game of pickup basketball, Yo-Yo's fellow campers at Meadowmount had thought nothing of meeting for impromptu chamber sessions regardless of the hour. Further summers at the Marlboro Festival, where he again played with small groups of similarly inclined musicians, only served to intensify his affection.

Not all great soloists make good chamber players. German poet Johann Wolfgang von Goethe once called chamber music "a discourse between reasonable individuals." The trappings of fame often strip away the elements of reasonableness and replace them with the desire to monopolize the spotlight. Such a desire is anathema to successful chamber music, in which every player has a clearly defined and equal role.

"He makes sure that the word soloist doesn't mean that he is a separate entity, that he just plays to the public and the hell with everyone else," Baltimore Symphony principal cellist Mihaly Virizlay said with reference to Yo-Yo. "We all join him in a joint venture."[7]

While Virizlay was referring to the attitude that Yo-Yo projects to the members of a large symphony, it is equally true of his approach to chamber music. It is perhaps one of Yo-Yo's greatest attributes that he has formed successful chamber music groups with so many different players. One of the first such groups was the trio at Harvard, consisting of Yo-Yo, Lynn Chang, and Richard Kogan, which continued after all three had graduated. Kogan explained one reason for this group's longevity, which also echoed Goethe's comment: "Yo-Yo really is more generous, less self-absorbed than other people. People who don't know him well think it's an act, but we know he's really like that."[8]

Of course, his long-standing collaboration with Manny Ax continues to be one of classical music's most durable pairings. He and Ax have made numerous appearances and recordings with Stern and Laredo besides that foursome's 1991 Grammy-winning album. At one point, Yo-Yo formed a string quartet with violinists Gidon Kremer and Daniel Phillips, and violist Kim Kashkashian. "We liked to do the last opus quartets, and the long ones; that was our specialty," he said. "If we had to find a name for ourselves, it would have been The Quartet that Plays Only the Late Works."[9]

Not long after pocketing his Grammys for his 1992 recordings at the award ceremonies in late February, 1993, Yo-Yo headed for another kind of chamber music concert. This one would be different from anything he had ever done. Very different.

NOTES

1. Richard Dyer, "Ma and McFerrin: A Match Made in Tanglewood," *Boston Globe*, January 19, 1991.

2. Joshua Kosman, "35 Who Made a Difference: Yo-Yo Ma," *Smithsonian* (November 2005).

3. Richard Dyer, "McFerrin and Ma: Concerts to Remember," *Boston Globe*, January 22, 1991.

4. Ed Siegel, "Playing the Full Human Range: Yo-Yo Ma Plays the Cello to Create a Portrait of the Artist," *Boston Globe*, August 6, 1995.

5. Linda Sanders, "Music Capsule Review: Hush; Play (1992)," *Entertainment Weekly*, March 6, 1992, http://www.ew.com/ew/article/0,,309794,00.html.

6. Richard Dyer, "Odd Couples: As Record Companies Strive to Match the Success of the Three Tenors Album, They Offer Celebrity Pairings That Range From the Memorable to the Purely Commercial," *Boston Globe*, March 15, 1992.

7. Justin Davidson, "Have Cello, Will Travel: For the tireless Yo-Yo Ma, All the World's an Audience," *Newsday*, November 30, 1997.

8. Evan Eisenberg, "Music; Through College and Life, In Harmony," *New York Times*, July 15, 2001.

9. Edith Eisler, "Yo-Yo Ma: Music from the Soul," *Strings* (May/June 1992).

Chapter 11

AMERICA MEETS AFRICA

During his extensive performing career, Yo-Yo had become accustomed to rapturous applause at the end of his concerts. Frequently his audiences had risen to their feet in spontaneous, long-lasting, and thoroughly heart-felt standing ovations.

But early in 1993, he encountered an entirely different reaction. He had performed for a small group in the type of intimate setting that fostered rapport between musician and audience. When he finished, his audience laughed at him.

Had the chorus of the signature song of the rock band America gone through his head at this moment it would have been fitting. He had indeed "been through the desert"—in this case, the inhospitable Kalahari Desert that links the countries of Botswana and Namibia in southwestern Africa (and had enjoyed considerable fame as the setting of the 1980 film *The Gods Must Be Crazy*). To the Bushmen who lived there, he was literally "A Horse [the meaning of his last name in Chinese] with No Name."

Never mind that elsewhere in the world he was regarded as one of the finest classical musicians. To the Bushmen, he was just a man who had somewhat mysteriously appeared in their midst, then fumbled his way through an attempt to play the *gwashi* (one of their musical instruments) as they watched with considerable amusement. It was a humorous situation. So they laughed.

In a sense, Yo-Yo's presence in the Kalahari was finally scratching a 20-year-old itch. While he was at Harvard, he had particularly enjoyed professor Irven DeVore's anthropology courses. DeVore had firsthand experience of the Bushmen, having lived among them for a substantial amount of time. He wasn't the only outsider to have done so. As one of the last groups of hunter/gatherers in the world, the Bushmen were of particular interest to anthropologists. Several anthropologists had made films.

An important element of DeVore's class involved watching those films. One in particular had a profound impact on Yo-Yo. Called *Bitter Melons*, its focus was a blind man named Ukzone. He sang songs about different aspects of the daily life of the Bushmen, using his hunting bow for instrumental accompaniment. He rested it on an overturned metal bowl—which he often struck to add a percussive element to his music—while plucking it with the fingers of both hands. The film was named for one of those songs, which described the bitter taste of melons in the wild. Yet, the song explains, these melons were essential for desert survival; during periods of particular aridity, they were a primary source of water.

Within Yo-Yo, the Bushmen's music struck a deep, responsive chord. He decided that he wanted to experience it firsthand. He was particularly interested in seeing if he could "find out where their music comes from, why they play it, and whether I would find any common ground between us."[1]

He also wanted to record his experiences there. He found a British television company, Skyline Productions, that was willing to work with him and that eventually would make a film entitled *Distant Echoes: Yo-Yo Ma and the Kalahari Bushmen*. In 1993 he flew to the Kalahari with Richard Lee, a colleague of DeVore's who was also an expert on the Bushmen, and the Skyline Productions film crew. The following two weeks were among the most important of his life—and, at least initially, among the most uneasy.

"You see a lot of sky, and you don't see people for days," he said in retrospect. "It's very scary."[2]

Once he got down to business, however, any qualms quickly vanished. He asked to see the various instruments the Bushmen used to make music. His hosts quickly obliged. They brought the hunting bows that had made such a memorable impression on him as he sat in DeVore's darkened classroom. They also introduced him to the *gwashi*. About a foot long and bearing a resemblance to a harp, it was made entirely of local materials: chunks of wood, dried animal skins, twigs, tree sap, and other natural items. The "strings" were actually stretched-out animal tendons. Yo-Yo couldn't resist trying to play it, accompanied by good-natured laughter from his audience. He also tried the *venturo*, what he regarded as the Bushmen version of the cello. It consists of an empty oil can and a single metal string. The player uses a twig for the bow. After several tries Yo-Yo was able to coax some meaningful notes out of it.

Then he reverted to his comfort zone. First he encouraged the villagers to try playing the cello he had brought with him (very likely neither the Montagnana nor the Davidov Strad). Then he played some Bach for them.

Almost immediately he sensed the unfitness of his instrument to the context of the millennia-old Kalahari Bushman society. "Such a booming sound," he noted. "Bach seems so young here, old by my standards, but compared to the Bushmen's cultural history [Lee believes that ancient Bushman wall paintings are at least 40,000 years old], it's no more than an instant."[3]

Perhaps the high point of his visit was watching the trance dance, one of the central rituals of the Bushmen. Many bush people walked for miles to participate. Accompanied by the complicated rhythms of drummers, with singing and clapping by the women (and on this occasion, Yo-Yo as well), the men danced for hours during the evening in a tight-knit circle around a large bonfire with rattles attached to their legs. Finally one man collapsed, trembling and shaking in a trance-like state. He was immediately proclaimed the village shaman, who would serve as the healer for the community.

Yo-Yo was deeply moved by what he had witnessed, later calling it a "synthesis of music and religion, a meditation, a gift from heaven."[4] DeVore, his Harvard professor, agreed. "It's one of the most impressive things a human will ever see,"[5] he said.

On his final day among the Bushmen, Yo-Yo hosted a party for the people with whom he had stayed, to thank them for their hospitality. Before the trip, he had put considerable time and effort into learning Hungarian composer Zoltán Kodály's Sonata for Solo Cello. Because it is based on folk melodies, Yo-Yo thought it would be appropriate to play as a sort of going-away present for his hosts.

Many musicians place Sonata for Solo Cello on the same plane of technical virtuosity and accomplishment as the Bach suites, and some maintain that at its composition in 1915 it was the most important composition of its kind since the Bach suites almost exactly two centuries earlier. Noted cellist Carlos Prieto calls it "incomparable" and "a work that takes full advantage of the instrument's tonal and expressive potential."[6] Edith Eisler would later write of Yo-Yo's 2006 recording that he "gives the fiendishly difficult Kodály sonata—with its incredible sound effects and fireworks—musical and emotional expression, making it sing, speak, shout, whisper, dance, and cry."[7] A performance of this work by Yo-Yo at Carnegie Hall or Avery Fisher Hall would almost certainly have attracted turnaway crowds.

But the Kalahari Desert wasn't New York City. The Bushmen would have none of it.

"They said, 'Stop. Don't play. We want to play for you,'" he laughed. "It was hubris on my part to bring my cello. They didn't give a damn."[8] Instead, the village musicians played a farewell "concert" for him. Yo-Yo's long hours of rehearsal went for naught, at least for the time being.

The same could hardly be said for his trip. "It changed my life," he said. "This is what the Beethoven Ninth is about. You get to the same place, the brotherhood of man."[9]

And later, he added, "I participated in their transcendent practices, dancing for hours in a circle around the fire. I listened to the old-style music, with people playing for the hunt, for prayer, and for art. That experience was more powerful than almost anything I've done. I asked a woman, 'Why do you do this?' She said, 'It gives us meaning.' How cool is that? That's as good a reason as any to do something."[10]

NOTES

1. Andrew L. Pincus, *Musicians with a Mission: Keeping the Classical Tradition Alive* (Boston: Northeastern University Press, 2002), p. 27.

2. Justin Davidson, "Have Cello, Will Travel: For the Tireless Yo-Yo Ma, All the World's an Audience," *Newsday*, November 30, 1997.

3. Janet Tassel, "Yo-Yo Ma's Journey," *Harvard Magazine*, March–April 2000.

4. Ibid.

5. Ibid.

6. Carlos Prieto, *The Adventures of a Cello*, translated by Elena C. Murray (Austin, Tex.: Texas University Press, 2006), p. 264.

7. Edith Eisler, "Yo-Yo Ma: Solo," http://www.amazon.ca/Solo-Mark-OConnor/dp/B00000K4II7.

8. Davidson, "Have Cello, Will Travel."

9. Pincus, *Musicians with a Mission*, p. 29.

10. Dorinda Elliott, "A Conversation with Yo-Yo Ma," *Conde Nast Traveler*, May, 2007.

Chapter 12

THE FREE-RANGE CELLIST

As the film *Distant Echoes: Yo-Yo Ma and the Kalahari Bushmen* approaches its end, Yo-Yo looks into the camera and announces that his sojourn among the Bushmen has inspired him to try out more forms of music—as if he hadn't already been doing that for several years. The Kalahari trip spurred him on to even greater efforts in that direction, so much so that a few years later he joked to a Honolulu reporter, on the eve of a concert appearance there, that "Musically, I'm a free-range chicken, a free range cellist, that's me."[1]

One of his departures from the beaten path had its origin in an encounter during the 80th birthday party for Stéphane Grappelli in 1988. There Yo-Yo met fiddler Mark O'Connor, who had performed regularly with Grappelli for several years. Yo-Yo was thoroughly impressed with O'Connor's style of playing. The timing was fortuitous. Yo-Yo was on the verge of expanding his musical horizons and was eager to learn the basics of country-style music.

He would have been hard-pressed to find a better teacher. As journalist Tony Scherman would later write, O'Connor was well on his way to establishing "one of the most spectacular, if underpublicized, journeys in recent American music."[2]

Born into a Seattle family plagued by alcoholism and illness in 1961, O'Connor began playing the guitar at the age of six as a means of coping with his turmoil at home. Four years later he won a local guitar competition, defeating a number of adults.

When he was 12 he met noted fiddler Benny Thomasson, and immediately started learning to play the violin. He quickly displayed the same precocious talent that had already been evident in his guitar work. He won several regional and national fiddling championships and recorded four albums by the time he graduated from high school. In the early 1980s, he demonstrated his Midas touch with new instruments by taking up the mandolin and quickly winning the World Mandolin Championship. He became well-established both as a studio musician and as a member of several highly regarded groups such as Grappelli's.

By the time he met Yo-Yo, O'Connor was becoming tired of the relatively simple melodies inherent in the folk and country styles that had been his meat and potatoes for the past decade. Soon afterward he set out in yet another direction when he began composing and playing classical music, often appearing as a violin soloist. His diverse background, and the similarity of his personality to Yo-Yo's—notably in the lack of an overbearing ego—signified that the two men could work well together.

O'Connor and Yo-Yo had such busy schedules that it took them years to hook up. They finally began rehearsing on a regular basis in 1994. They were joined by bass player Edgar Meyer, who also had a particularly distinguished resume in both folk and classical music. The trio were not in agreement about the quality of their initial efforts. While Yo-Yo was pleased with their results, his partners weren't. For one of the few times in his career, Yo-Yo found himself the low man on the totem pole.

"I could see that [Mark] wasn't happy with what was coming out of my cello," Yo-Yo said. "Edgar is more verbal, and he could explain what specifically I was doing wrong. It took me a long time to satisfy them."[3]

Yo-Yo didn't give up, and in time he reached the exacting standards of his partners. The three men began appearing in concert together the following year and released *Appalachia Waltz* in 1996. The album is a nod in the direction of American folk music, in particular the rich lode of melodies originating in the Appalachian Mountains that extend from the state of New York to Alabama. Several of the songs are arrangements of traditional tunes. O'Connor and Meyer both wrote additional original material. The result was a fusion of classical and folk styles. *Appalachia Waltz* shot to the top of the Billboard crossover chart, stayed there for several months, and remained a fixture on lower rungs of the chart for a year and a half.

A different project took Yo-Yo from the mountains of Appalachia to the pampas of Argentina. His always-curious mind had developed an interest in tango music, in particular music composed by Astor Piazzolla.

Piazzolla was born in Argentina in 1921 and his family soon moved to New York. Unlike Yo-Yo, Casals, and others whose musical destinies were determined by receiving a musical instrument they wanted, Piazzolla's path began at the age of eight when his father presented him with an instrument he definitely didn't want. At that time, he had his heart set on a pair of roller skates and had long made his feelings clear. So when his father came home one day with a package for him, young Astor couldn't have been happier—until he opened it.

"It was a letdown because instead of a pair of skates, I found an artifact I had never seen before in my life," he recounted. "Dad sat down, set it on my legs, and told me, 'Astor, this is the instrument of tango. I want you to learn it.'"[4]

The instrument was a bandoneón, similar to an accordion but having dozens of buttons instead of keys. His father, homesick for the tango music of his native Argentina, had found it in a pawnshop. Piazzolla didn't realize it, but he had just begun one of the most fascinating stories in modern music annals.

Despite his initial misgivings, he began playing the instrument and soon became adept. A few years later, a piano-playing neighbor introduced him to Bach, a change that was to have long-lasting implications. In addition to his new interest in Bach, his American sojourn also gave him an enduring appreciation and love for jazz. While Astor was still a teenager, the family returned to Argentina. He soon made his living playing and composing tango music. But—at least in part because of his strong feelings for Bach—he felt that his destiny lay in classical composition.

The turning point in Piazzolla's career came in 1954 when he was studying music composition in Paris with the legendary composer and conductor Nadia Boulanger. Boulanger's associations included French classical composer Maurice Ravel, and American classical composers Aaron Copland and Leonard Bernstein. Piazzolla concealed his tango background from her because he was deeply ashamed of it. She was unimpressed with his classical compositions, and finally he revealed the folk element of his musical background. Intrigued, she asked him to play one of his tango compositions.

"When I finished Nadia took my hands in hers and with that English of hers, so sweet, she said, 'Astor, this is beautiful, I really like it a lot. Here is the true Piazzolla—don't ever leave him,'" he recalled several decades later. "It was the great revelation of my musical life."[5]

When he returned home, Piazzolla drew on elements of his jazz and classical background to begin composing what he called the "new tango." Structured around the bandoneón, the music he produced bewildered his countrymen. It may have been the "real Piazzolla" but to them it was not "real tango." He received a great deal of criticism, even death threats. ("I love that," Yo-Yo commented when he heard of the death threats. "Imagine people caring so much about music!"[6])

In spite of the opposition from some of his countrymen, Piazzolla's music thrived. At one point, he wrote *Le Grand Tango*, a composition for cello and piano that he dedicated to Rostropovich. By the time of his death in 1992, he was almost universally regarded as the most important figure in tango music.

In light of Piazzolla's multigenre musical background, it is not surprising that Yo-Yo eventually became one of his greatest champions. Yo-Yo's interest in Piazzolla, and in tango music as a genre, took some time to develop. Though he ardently studied both the composer and the history and culture of Argentina, he commented with regard to Piazzolla's music that, "I loved it, but I didn't get it."[7]

A trip to Argentina opened his eyes. During his visit, he happened to go into a bar where a 90-year-old man was pounding out passionate tango melodies on a piano. "Oh my God, *that's* what they're playing," he said. "It's giant!"[8]

Back home, he quickly put what he had just learned to good use. He contributed to the soundtrack of the 1997 film, *The Tango Lesson*. More important, he made *Soul of the Tango*, an album in which he collaborated with some of the best-known tango musicians in the world. One track, "Tango Remembrances," posthumously included Piazzolla himself. Through the magic of modern sound recording, Yo-Yo electronically spanned a decade of time as he played along with a recording that Piazzolla had made in 1987.

Listeners and critics loved *Soul of the Tango*. The album won Yo-Yo his 13th Grammy, this one in the Classical Crossover category.

Yo-Yo's penchant for commissioning new works also moved into high gear after his Kalahari expedition. The year 1994 alone resulted in several new concertos written at his request: by Richard Danielpour, John Harbison, and Christopher Rouse.

That same year he released *New York Album*. The name came from the fact that the three works on the album—by Stephen Albert, Béla Bartók, and Ernest Bloch—had all been composed in New York over a span of more than 70 years.

Yo-Yo was of course very familiar with the Albert Cello Concerto, having premiered it in 1990. The Bartók work, on the other hand, required Yo-Yo to learn a new instrument. The Hungarian-born composer had become world-renowned before fleeing Hungary in 1940 as war clouds grew over Europe. Bartók settled in New York. He died five years later, leaving his final work, the Viola Concerto, unfinished. A student of his finished it in 1949. Yo-Yo played it using an alto violin (sometimes also referred to as a vertical viola), an instrument about midway in size between a viola and a cello. While some people played it under their chin, the more common practice, which Yo-Yo adopted, was to insert a particularly long end pin and play the instrument seated, in the same manner as a cello.

The third work on *New York Album* was Bloch's *Schelomo: Hebraic Rhapsody for Violoncello and Orchestra*. This piece had been composed in 1916 and drew on Bloch's Jewish heritage. It was based on the biblical story of King Solomon, and had originally been conceived with a vocal part for the monarch. Cellist Alexandre Barjansky talked Bloch into giving the vocal part to the cello, and it became a favorite of cellists because of the intense emotion that Bloch conveys in the composition.

In view of the words "New York" in the title, it is ironic that Yo-Yo recorded the album in Baltimore, Maryland. However, he was working with the Baltimore Symphony and conductor David Zinman, thereby reuniting the same creative team that had resulted in a Grammy in 1989 for the concertos by Benjamin Britten and Samuel Barber. The team worked again: when the Grammys were awarded for 1994, *New York Album* won Yo-Yo the prize for Best Instrumental Soloist Performance with Orchestra. Albert was also honored posthumously with the award for Best Classical Contemporary Composition.

In January, 1996, Yo-Yo achieved a triple rarity—indeed, almost certainly doing something that had never been done before. He played three concertos in a single concert with Zinman and the Baltimore Symphony. Each concerto was written by a twentieth-century composer. And all three—by Richard Danielpour, Christopher Rouse, and Leon Kirchner—had been composed specifically with Yo-Yo in mind.

The Kirchner concerto had a story behind it that was awash with Harvard connections. For starters, of course, Kirchner had been Yo-Yo's mentor—and sometime harsh critic—while Yo-Yo was a student there. In addition, fellow Harvard alum Cathy Barbash had been the manager of the Harvard-Radcliffe Orchestra during a 1971 performance when Yo-Yo, at that time still in high school, played with the orchestra as a soloist. Barbash's parents, Lillian and Maurice, were in the audience, and through the succeeding years, the elder Barbashes—who were very active in promoting music in the New York area—followed Yo-Yo's career closely.

When the Barbashes' 40th wedding anniversary approached in 1987, they weren't sure how they wanted to celebrate the occasion. The answer came one day while they were driving and talking about the upcoming event, meanwhile listening to their car radio. Maurice recalled later that he asked Lillian, "Do you want to have a party?" Maurice went on to explain, "Just then the music ended and the announcer said, 'That was

Dumbarton Oaks by Stravinsky, commissioned by Mr. So-and-So in honor of his and his wife's anniversary.'"

"'That's what I want!' Lillian replied. 'I'd like to commission a concerto for Yo-Yo Ma.'"[9]

While Yo-Yo was very receptive to the idea, he cautioned the Barbashes about the very possible one-and-done fate of many commissions: After their premieres, they are never performed again. It was a risk the Barbashes were willing to take. "At least we'd have a tape to pass on to our grandchildren,"[10] Lillian said.

Yo-Yo asked them who they wanted to compose it. They shrugged their shoulders. They weren't familiar with twentieth-century composers, at least ones who were still alive. They left the choice to Yo-Yo, and he picked Kirchner. The composition proved to be anything but an overnight process. Riccardo Muti and the Philadelphia Orchestra finally premiered what Kirchner had entitled Music for Cello and Orchestra in 1992, shortly before the Barbashes celebrated not their 40th, but their 45th anniversary.

The wait was worth it. The concerto proved to be much more than a simple one-and-done. Two years after the premiere, the work won the Friedheim Award, given annually by the John F. Kennedy Center for the Performing Arts to honor outstanding instrumental compositions by American composers. Given the fact that Yo-Yo and his sister had assisted in the 1962 fundraiser that helped provide initial funding for the Kennedy Center, the award seemed especially appropriate.

When Yo-Yo decided to perform the Kirchner as part of the 1996 concert triple-header, he threw in an extra bonus for the Barbashes. Along with the other two works, the Kirchner would be recorded for a new album, *Yo-Yo Ma Premieres*.

The program was performed live twice, on Friday and Saturday. Yo-Yo and the orchestra spent much of the time between the two concerts recording the first concerto, the Danielpour.

Early the following morning, a blizzard dumped several feet of snow on the East Coast and paralyzed traffic. Zinman fretted that the project could be delayed, perhaps for a matter of years, or it could be canceled altogether because of tight time commitments for many of the principals involved and the difficulty of getting them together again. Fortunately, nearly all of the musicians—many of whom lived miles from the recording studio—braved the massive snowdrifts and showed up at the studio two days later.

In liner notes to the album, Zinman said, "The Barbashes arrive to root for the Kirchner. We all want this to go well, because this is the work that started the whole project and Yo-Yo especially wants to please Leon, his former Harvard professor."[11]

It did go well, and the Barbashes, whose expectations had by now been fulfilled many times over, had still another surprise in store. In February the following year, they were skiing in Taos, New Mexico, when Yo-Yo sent them a fax.

"There was just one fax machine at the post office and two sisters who ran it," Maurice said. "And one comes running up to us with the fax in her hand, which of course she had read. She said, is this from the real Yo-Yo Ma?"[12]

It was indeed from the real Yo-Yo Ma, and it contained astonishing news: The album had won a Grammy award! Actually, it had done better than that. It had won two. One was specifically for Yo-Yo, honoring him as Best Instrumental Soloist Performance with Orchestra. The other was even better: Zinman and Yo-Yo, along with producer Steven Epstein, got the nod for Best Classical Album.

In spite of the recognition conferred on them by winning the Grammy, the three composers on the album were hardly household words. But the situation was far different for another composer with whom Yo-Yo had also collaborated during 1994, his watershed year for new works: John Williams.

Williams was born in 1932. He studied piano at Juilliard in the mid-1950s and began working with composer Henry Mancini on a number of scores for popular television series. He branched out on his own a few years later, and his first Academy Award nomination came in 1967 for *Valley of the Dolls*. Four years later he took home his first Oscar for his film adaptation of the score of *Fiddler on the Roof*.

In 1974 he began working with then relatively unknown American film director Stephen Spielberg. Their second film, *Jaws*, became a huge success. Williams won an Oscar for his score and the film's music is still instantly recognizable, especially his two-note shark motif. Williams went on to create dozens of additional memorable movie scores, including *Star Wars*, the *Indiana Jones* series, *ET: The Extraterrestrial*, *Close Encounters of the Third Kind*, *Jurassic Park* and many others. He also composed "Olympic Fanfare and Theme" in 1984, which NBC Sports has used during its Olympics coverage since then.

In addition to his extraordinary popular success, Williams also was the conductor of the Boston Pops Orchestra between 1980 and 1993, and composed a number of classical works. He and Yo-Yo met at Tanglewood shortly after Yo-Yo's return from his Kalahari trip. Williams conducted the Boston Symphony Orchestra in a performance of the Elgar Cello Concerto, with Yo-Yo as the soloist. The two men struck up an instant friendship, which resulted in Williams' composition, Concerto for Cello and Orchestra. Williams conducted the BSO and Yo-Yo was soloist when the work premiered at the opening of the Seiji Ozawa Hall in Tanglewood the following year.

The two men hooked up again three years later when Williams wrote the score for the film *Seven Years in Tibet*, which starred Brad Pitt. Yo-Yo was featured on the soundtrack.

By that time Yo-Yo was no stranger to film work. In 1994, he joined forces with Ax and violinist Pamela Frank to play one of Beethoven's piano trios as part of the soundtrack for *Immortal Beloved*, a fictionalized account of an important part of Beethoven's life. Yo-Yo also played a prominent role in the soundtrack of the 1997 PBS production of *Liberty!*, a documentary account of the Revolutionary War. He was particularly attracted to the project because his friend Mark O'Connor composed part of the soundtrack and adapted some folk songs of that era.

That same year, Yo-Yo joined Chinese composer Tan Dun in the 1997 Symphony, written to celebrate the unification of Hong Kong with China. It was a massive work, lasting well over an hour, and similar to Beethoven's Ninth Symphony (of which it contained a brief motif) in that it featured a chorus, written in this case for a children's choir. The work also had a major role for solo cello. Yo-Yo was the obvious choice for the recording, which was issued at about the same time that the work premiered in Hong Kong that year.

Still another major project was finally coming to fruition at about the same time. Collaborations were one thing. His solo career was another. The six Bach cello suites had always been an important part of his life. Perhaps influenced by his experiences in the Kalahari, he had begun thinking of making a new recording soon after his return. But Yo-Yo being Yo-Yo, he was thinking of doing something beyond a recording. His close association with the camera crew during his stint in the Kalahari Desert had given him an inspiration—for Bach.

NOTES

1. Tim Ryan, "Yo! Cellist Extraordinaire Yo-Yo Ma Reveals His Secret to Balance in his Life," *Honolulu Star-Bulletin*, March 16, 1999.

2. Tony Scherman, "Music: Fiddling While the Old Barriers Burn," *New York Times*, April 2, 2000.

3. Edith Eisler, "Continuity in Diversity," *Strings*, May–June 2001.

4. Natalio Gorin, *Astor Piazzolla: A Memoir*, translated, annotated, and expanded by Fernando Gonzalez (Portland, Ore.: Amadeus Press, 2001), p. 141.

5. Ibid.

6. Justin Davidson, "Have Cello, Will Travel: For the Tireless Yo-Yo Ma, All the World's an Audience," *Newsday*, November 30, 1997.

7. Dorinda Elliott, "A Conversation with Yo-Yo Ma," *Conde Nast Traveler*, May 2007.

8. Ibid.

9. "Meet the Composer—The Insider's Scoop, Lillian & Maurice Barbash," http://www.meetthecomposer.org/indguide/barbash.html.

10. Ibid.

11. Andrew L. Pincus, *Musicians with a Mission: Keeping the Classical Tradition Alive* (Boston: Northeastern University Press, 2002), p. 24.

12. "Meet the Composer."

Chapter 13

YO-YO MA AND THE SUITE LIFE

The idea that would eventually emerge as the six-film series *Inspired by Bach*—one of Yo-Yo's major undertakings—had its genesis in October 1991. Yo-Yo was invited to join a symposium in Boston on the life and works of Albert Schweitzer, one of the great humanitarians of the twentieth century. Schweitzer, who won the Nobel Peace Prize in 1952, was most noted for establishing a hospital in the African country of Gabon in 1913 and devoting the rest of his life to maintaining it.

Before turning to medicine, however, Schweitzer had been an accomplished organist, so renowned that he later gave concerts to help provide funding for his hospital. He was also one of the world's leading authorities on Bach and had written extensively about him. As a result, many of the discussions at the symposium revolved around Bach and how it was impossible to completely describe everything about him.

In preparation for his appearance, Yo-Yo reread a number of Schweitzer's works. He was especially interested in Schweitzer's description of Bach as a "pictorial composer." That is, Bach's music was rich in visual imagery in addition to its profoundly moving sonic qualities.

Yo-Yo derived another insight from the symposium. The other participants included doctors, social workers, and theologians. Their separate fields of life work involved attempting feats that were as impossible as completely describing Bach. Not all patients could be cured. Not everyone could have a comfortable home. Not everyone could become spiritually whole. But making efforts in that direction gave meaning to these dedicated people's lives.

The following year, Yo-Yo took part in another series of discussions, "The Spiritual Beauty of Bach," which were part of the Tanglewood Festival. His participation required Yo-Yo to reexamine his understanding of Bach. A good portion of this reexamination revolved around the six suites for solo cello, which he presented in another marathon, single-evening recital at the festival.

His previous recording of the six suites was now nearly 10 years behind him. His understanding of himself, of Bach, and of the suites themselves had undergone numerous changes. One change, perhaps brought into sharper focus by the Schweitzer conference the previous year, was that he now saw music as an important way to comfort others. Music could be "a healing thing for people going through tough times,"[1] he said.

Another change, also illustrated at the conference, lay in his perception of what the suites were attempting in contrast to what they could in fact accomplish. Yo-Yo realized that in the suites Bach too was trying something impossible. Unlike the organ with its multiple keyboards and pedals, the cello was capable only of a single melodic line. Yet Bach was trying to use the instrument to create polyphony.

Finally, Yo-Yo realized that there was another impossibility. No single performer could exhaust all the meanings inherent in the material. He later remembered concluding, "I can't own it. And so I thought, 'I can spend all my life playing it and I can just report my experience or my knowledge of it.'"[2]

That thought led to still another insight: "Suppose we regard a piece of music as almost genetic material, like DNA, to the mind of a person who is both very receptive and imaginative. How would that person think of it, not in terms of the cello, but of their own medium?"[3]

Yo-Yo envisioned producing each suite in collaboration with someone in an entirely different discipline. This person would interpret that suite in his or her own idiom and produce a visual accompaniment to Yo-Yo's music. The suites would thus present two layers of meaning, in effect creating the polyphony that Bach had striven for.

In Yo-Yo's mind, *Inspired by Bach* was a daring departure from his comfort zone. He knew that the project would take years to come to its final fruition.

He chose Canadian-based Rhombus Media to produce the project. The company was especially noted for its 1993 film, *Thirty Two Short Films About Glenn Gould*. Gould was a famous, somewhat eccentric Canadian pianist who carved out a stellar performing and recording career before his untimely death in 1982 at the age of 50. He was especially noted for his interpretations of Bach.

Yo-Yo and Rhombus proved to be a good pairing. Rhombus became totally involved in the production, providing directors for several of the individual films. Through the Gould project these directors had also become familiar with Bach's life and works in general, so they brought an especially appropriate body of knowledge to the enterprise.

The first film, set to Suite No. 1 in G Major, is titled *Music Garden*. Though it began as a work of the imagination, it depicts an actual series of events. It opens with an image of an unfolding rose, reflecting Yo-Yo's belief that this suite is about nature. In the film, Yo-Yo joins forces with real-life noted landscape architect Julie Moir Messervy to design a garden at Boston's City Hall Plaza. Located in the heart of the city and surrounded by government buildings, the nine-acre site seems barren and arid. Messervy wants to change that impression by planting trees, flowers, and other plants, and thereby provide an urban oasis in accord with her interpretation of each of the six movements of the suite.

At first Boston officials are welcoming and optimistic. Mayor Thomas Menino thanks Yo-Yo for his vision, then appears before television cameras to tell Bostonians that he thinks the music garden is a fabulous idea.

During the opening moments of the suite, the camera continually juxtaposes images of Yo-Yo playing his cello in various points in the existing space of City Hall Plaza, and then in open fields among trees, flowers, and plants. At one point, time-lapse photography shows tree trunks and hedges replacing the sterile concrete pillars that surround Yo-Yo as he plays, a tantalizing hint of what could be.

Next the film shows brief interviews with civic leaders, some of whom begin expressing skepticism about the viability of the project and the difficulties of raising enough money. One says that theme gardens always fail. Another sighs as he says that "artists just have different views than we do."

In the script, the project nonetheless moves forward. Messervy and city technicians begin conducting preliminary studies of the soil beneath the plaza's primary architectural feature, its 1,246,343 paving stones. Near the end of the courante, the suite's third movement, the camera swirls ever faster around Yo-Yo as he sits in the midst of a garden in full flower and butterflies alight on the strings of his cello. Then the front page of a newspaper floats gently to the ground. The camera zooms in to the shocking headline: "Ma's Music Garden Plan Falls Through."

The succeeding image is of a Boston official, who explains that the city had to be practical and cancel the project because the plan had become "too complex."

Cut to the sarabande, the fourth movement, which opens with light filtering through a forest glade. Yo-Yo explains that he knew the project would be hard, which was fitting. The suites are also hard, he comments, including his now-familiar statement that Bach was trying to create polyphony with a single line of music.

Messervy is more literal. Saying that she smiled "far too much" trying to get things done, she adds that the failure was a case of two worldviews that couldn't come together. Yes, she adds, the outcome made her angry and bitter.

These feelings don't last long. The city of Toronto, Canada, is interested in the project.

Once again, the initial reception is positive. Once again, the mayor is on board with the idea. Once again, the aridity of the site is clearly revealed. Standing in its midst, Messervy says, "All I can see are cement mixers, cranes, an overhead highway. I need to be imaginative."

The film depicts her stream of imagination: footage of concrete being broken up, then time-lapse photography showing grass and ferns sprouting, branches budding, and leaves unfolding.

The next step is raising money. Toronto mayor Barbara Hall has already set the tone by telling people that the garden will generate excitement and bring people together. Because the proposed site, on the shores of Lake Ontario next to a small boat marina, is smaller than Boston's City Hall Plaza, the expenses aren't as great. Several civic leaders express optimism that they can raise the necessary funds. At a party for would-be donors, Yo-Yo plays the cello and explains that the garden will in effect become a concert hall without walls.

In the final movement of the suite, the gigue, Mayor Hall expresses confidence that the park will be built. And it seems evident that Yo-Yo is a significant part of the project's success—that he's done a considerable amount of schmoozing and chatting up potential donors. "If anything happens to the cello, I'll get you a sales and marketing job," a man tells him.

The movement—and the film—come to an end with Yo-Yo playing in a large tent on the site in another event for donors. The mood is buoyant.

"I'm moved to be here in front of you," he says to his audience. "It's taken a long time but it's really been worth it."

The camera pulls away from him, moves outside, and slowly withdraws from the tent to reveal the outlines of several of the paths that will wind through the park. The promise is clear: The Toronto Music Garden will soon come into existence.

Of the six films, *Music Garden* had by far the most enduring aftermath. As the closing scenes suggested, the park in Toronto was indeed built. Its construction benefited from some good timing. In 1999, Yo-Yo won the Glenn Gould Prize, which is awarded every three years to a person who has made particularly distinguished contributions to music. Yo-Yo immediately donated the $50,000 that accompanied the award to help in building the park. Today, it is open daily and hosts concerts, weddings, and other activities that range from rock climbing to mountain biking. Many people come just to spend time wandering through it, gaining inspiration and a respite from the stress of daily life. It receives prominent mention in Toronto city guidebooks and reflects Messervy's vision.

Toronto's gain was definitely Boston's loss. Many of the city's citizens realized the opportunity they had squandered as icy blasts continued to sweep across the plaza's barren spaces during the winter. One city official even compared losing the park with losing its most famous baseball player, Babe Ruth, to New York and setting off the famous "curse of the Bambino." It took Boston 86 years to overcome that curse and win the World Series. While City Hall Plaza is not that old, it has its own "curse": In 2004 the Project for Public Spaces ranked City Hall Plaza number one in its list of the world's worst public squares and plazas. Little in its design has changed since then.

The second film, *The Sound of the Carceri*, focuses on the works of Italian architect Giovanni Piranesi, who was born in 1720. The choice of an architect as the subject may owe its genesis to Goethe's observation that architecture is "frozen music." Early in the film, Yo-Yo makes it clear that the film's intention is to explore the relationship between the two forms of human expression, music and architecture.

Even though Piranesi was trained as an architect, he was responsible for the construction of just a single building, the S. Maria del Priorato church in Rome. His fame rests primarily not on buildings, but on two sets of engravings. The first, *Vedute* (Views), is a series of well over a hundred etchings of Roman scenes. The other is *Carceri d'Invenzione* (Imaginary Prisons), a 16-plate series that he published in 1749–1750 and reissued in 1761. Both sets were characterized by viewpoints that emphasized the size of their subjects, and by a heightening of the contrast between light and shadow to increase their visual drama. Some of Piranesi's views of interlocking sets of stairs bear a passing resemblance to the works of twentieth-century Dutch graphic artist M. C. Escher.

The Sound of the Carceri, shot entirely in black and white, opens with a personal note from Yo-Yo. He explains that the prelude of the suite was the very first piece that he himself performed in public, when he was five years old. He further notes that the film will visually put him in a space that never existed, playing music that was never danced to. The film is therefore a work that has required a great deal of imagination to produce.

Yet the visual aspect of the film has to be firmly grounded in reality. Yo-Yo in reality plays in the church that Piranesi designed, though 3D computer animation places him in a huge vaulted room that comes straight from Piranesi's etchings. In sepia tones, the camera alternates among close-ups of Yo-Yo, cutaway shots that show the immensity of the room that dwarfs him, and further close-ups of prison apparatus: barred windows, sharp spikes, chains, grates, and a rack.

As the film's title implies, sound is of particular importance in its making. The film shows numerous interchanges between Yo-Yo and sound engineer Steven Epstein. The two men are constantly experimenting with various aspects of sound. Yo-Yo is often filmed sitting in the midst of a battery of microphones. Yo-Yo demonstrates how even slight movements of his cello's end pin, at one point a shift of just a quarter of an inch, will produce subtle nuances in tonal qualities. By the end of the filming Yo-Yo appears to have tired of the constant tinkering. After yet another discussion with Epstein, he sighs, then mutters, "Boy, I'll be here all night. Just want to get out of here."

Not all the interchanges depicted in the film involve Epstein. Several scholars and musicians also add commentary. One of the most interesting is composer Richard Danielpour, who discusses the D-minor key in which Bach's second suite for cello is written. He notes that this key denotes isolation, loneliness, and struggle, and observes that most of Beethoven's Ninth Symphony—which also deals with these issues before concluding with the magnificent "Ode to Joy"—is written in the same key. So is Bach's own *St. John Passion*. At one point in the *St. John Passion*, Jesus is led away in chains from the Garden of Gethsemane, echoing the themes of bondage and imprisonment that Piranesi expresses in the Carceri images.

This commentary returns the viewer to the theme of imagination. The film suggests that Piranesi created the prison images to reflect the imprisonment of his own imagination. He couldn't do what he probably most wanted to, which was to create real buildings. Instead, his imagination was contained, leading to frustration and angst.

As the final movement draws toward its end, the camera slowly pulls away from Yo-Yo, making him appear increasingly tiny in the midst of the vast reaches of Piranesi's imaginary vault. Eventually he disappears entirely and the sepia-toned computer image fades into a replica of Piranesi's original black-and-white engraving.

To produce Bach's third cello suite, No. 3 in C Major, Yo-Yo chose to work with modern dance choreographer Mark Morris. Like Yo-Yo, as a child Morris too had an "Aha!" moment that determined the course of his life. It came when he attended a performance by noted flamenco artist José Greco when he was eight. Morris began taking dance lessons soon afterward. He moved from his Seattle home to New York when he was 19.

Five years later, in 1980, he founded his own Brooklyn-based company, the Mark Morris Dance Group. He has been the company's artistic director ever since, during a career that includes his choreographing well over 100 original dances, collaborations with most of the big names in the field, and regional and national awards that include a number of honorary doctorates.

Although it is not evident in the film, Morris took a year to make up his mind about participating in *Inspired by Bach*. As he explains to Yo-Yo in one of the film's first scenes, "It's always dangerous to trust a piece of music to the opinion of a choreographer. It's easy to feel that I'm committing a crime against music. Here's this fabulous piece of music—isn't that enough?"

Eventually Yo-Yo convinced him otherwise. While Yo-Yo didn't cite Walt Whitman, the nineteenth-century poet's line, "I am large, I contain multitudes," from *Song of Myself* could be applied to the Bach suites. Even multiple approaches don't exhaust the multitude of ideas contained in them.

Yo-Yo also had to persuade the film's director, Barbara Willis Sweete, who had some initial misgivings about the validity of combining visual media with Bach's suites. "I was reassured by [Yo-Yo's] position that this music, great as it is, can thrive on being interpreted by infinite numbers of creative artists, whether they be musicians, dancers, or even filmmakers—and that even with all of these interpretations, only certain aspects of what this music is describing can ever be grasped," she said when the project was finished. "Bach's vision is so vast and all-encompassing that it could never be captured in its entirety."[4]

Morris's idea for the dance that appears in the film came to him one day during a sort of dream-like state. He envisioned a terrible accident in which one of his dancers fell down a flight of stairs. *Falling Down Stairs* took its genesis from that moment, and the film opens with a black-and-white shot of the entire company of 14 dancers falling down a set of risers. Of course they do it far more gracefully than in Morris's original trance.

The format of the films for the first two suites divided each movement into an initial discussion followed by Yo-Yo performing the music. This clearly wouldn't work in *Falling Down Stairs* as it would have interrupted the flow of the finished dance. So the "chatty" portion takes up the first half of the film. Numerous discussions between Yo-Yo and Morris appear interspersed with rehearsal scenes, in which Yo-Yo's obvious delight at watching the dancers is almost palpable.

Finally the rehearsals are finished. The entire company attends an outdoor picnic, after which they don their costumes—produced by another big name, noted fashion designer Isaac Mizrahi, who makes a cameo appearance—and then sounds the call inside the rehearsal space of "Positions, please." The scenery is spare: a set of risers at one end, with Yo-Yo sitting on a small pedestal at the other. This setting assures that both elements—the dancers and the musician—are equals. Such an equality is comparatively rare in dancing; most dances are performed either with the musicians nearly invisible in the orchestra pit in front of and below the stage, or with recorded music.

As Yo-Yo begins playing the prelude, all the dancers once again tumble gracefully down the steps onto the floor. The movement continues with the dancers rising, falling again, and punching their arms upward. The same elements occur frequently in the following five movements.

Perhaps the most interesting—and certainly the most humorous—is the bourrée (the galanterie, or folk-dance-inspired fifth movement of the suite, which Bach uses in this third suite and also in the fourth). The bourrée opens with a 1-2-3-2-1 diamond formation of dancers on the steps. After elaborate and synchronized movements in which hands, arms, and bodies twist from side to side, the dancers abruptly sit neatly in three rows of three on the steps and watch five dancers on the floor. At one point all nine dancers on the stairs lean back in unison. When the five floor dancers exit, the group on the risers get to their feet and repeat many of their earlier movements, still in their three parallel rows.

The dance—and the film—ends with the lively gigue that is the cello suite's final movement. Two or four dancers run up and down the stairs as the rest of the 13 swirl around on the floor, and at the end they form two parallel rows, dash toward the camera, and then peel off to either side.

While that moment was the end of the film, it was hardly the end of the dance. It became incorporated into the Morris company repertoire. Nor was it the end of collaborations between Yo-Yo and Morris. They worked together on *The Argument* (1999) and on *Kolam* (2002), which was part of the Silk Road Project.

To direct the fourth Bach cello suite, No. 4 in E-flat Major, Yo-Yo chose Canadian independent filmmaker Atom Egoyan. Egoyan, in turn, chose to develop a nearly hour-long movie. Its theme was established when Yo-Yo gave a private performance of the film for Egoyan, who was struck by how carefully Yo-Yo seemed to be regarding him while he was playing. He felt that Yo-Yo had established a relationship with him, one based on generosity and the willingness to give of himself. Egoyan therefore decided that his film in turn would be based on relationships.

The theme was further developed according to Egoyan's belief that Bach may have intended that his six suites, taken together, would reflect the same structure as each individual suite. That is, the first suite was the prelude, the second was the allemande, and so on. Therefore the fourth suite was the sarabande, and Egoyan gave his film that title.

Unlike the other films, however, there are no breaks between the suite's movements. They are woven into the film at various points and played in a variety of locations: in concert, in master classes, on the radio, even the back seat of a limousine.

As the film opens, a woman drives up to a house with a prominent For Sale sign. Her name is Sarah (which, given the title of the film, can hardly be an accidental name choice), and she is the realtor. She tells the house's owner, a dying physician named Cassowitz, that she has just received an offer from a potential buyer. After discussing some of the terms of the possible sale, he hands her two tickets for a live performance of Yo-Yo playing the Bach cello suites.

The next scene—a brief one—depicts Yo-Yo actually playing the suites at the concert Sarah attends. After that, Sammy, a limousine driver of Greek descent, waits impatiently at the airport for Yo-Yo. Other drivers easily find the passengers they are supposed to pick up. Not Sammy.

By now it is clear that Egoyan will constantly shift back and forth, both among his characters and in time. Other characters soon emerge—most notably Dr. France, the female physician who is taking over the practice of the dying Dr. Cassowitz, and Sarah's boyfriend. The rest of the film works out the interconnections among these characters.

For example, Sarah has been one of Dr. Cassowitz's patients. Now she is seeing Dr. France for the first time, and tells her that she has an annoying cough. The doctor can find nothing organically wrong with her and suggests a possible psychosomatic cause. Its likely cause becomes evident near the end of the film.

In the meantime, Yo-Yo's driver has managed to locate him. But now the limousine has become stuck in traffic. Increasingly concerned about his lack of preparation time before the concert, Yo-Yo begins playing his cello to warm up. When he pauses, Sammy engages him in conversation. Eventually they discuss the spiritual and healing powers of music. "You are an ambassador from God," Sammy tells him. Ever humble, Yo-Yo replies, "Let's not go too far."

But there definitely is a connection. Dr. France is an accomplished cellist who has taken several master classes with Yo-Yo. In fact, she decided to go into medicine after her first master class several years earlier when Yo-Yo asked her how best she could help people.

Because Egoyan sees the sarabande as a stately, introspective dance— even melancholy—the shadow of death permeates the film. Yet there is life as well. As Yo-Yo reaches the gigue, the final movement of the suite, he notes that it comes from a happy place, full of life. And at the end Sammy tells Yo-Yo that hearing him play has been "better than a whole Greek feast."

The film made around the fifth suite, No. 5 in C Minor, is entitled *Struggle for Hope*. To develop it, Yo-Yo turned to Japanese Kabuki actor Tamasaburo Bando. Yo-Yo enlisted the services of Bando for the same reason he had enlisted Morris: to create an original dance. Praising Bando, Yo-Yo comments that the actor "uses every gesture and nuance with exquisite command, using these features to express ideas, characters and feelings, in the same way that Bach might use melodic motifs to create a musical picture."

Yo-Yo had long admired Kabuki, the traditional and highly stylized Japanese theatrical form that links acting, dancing, and singing. The actors—all men, who play both male and female roles—wear elaborate, colorful costumes. These elements come together to create particularly compelling drama.

In the making of *Struggle for Hope*, not all the drama occurred in front of the camera. The film's production team was already in Japan and was only waiting for Yo-Yo's arrival to begin filming. But during a brief stopover in Detroit on his way there, Yo-Yo got a shocking phone call from director/producer Niv Fichman: Bando had just canceled the project. He didn't like the physical set. He had issues with Fichman's dual role. He was busy with another film project, in which he was the director.

Despite the bad news, Yo-Yo decided to continue the long flight. As the fundraising for the Toronto Music Garden had demonstrated, he has considerable persuasive powers. He closeted himself with Bando and convinced him not to back out. Even after Bando agreed to continue, making the film wasn't an easy process. The start of the project had to be postponed. Both Bando and Yo-Yo had packed schedules and their time together was minimal. As a result, Yo-Yo spent hours, often in hotel rooms while he was traveling to fulfill concert obligations, recording portions of the suite and adding his thoughts. He would send these recordings to Bando, who in turn would listen to them in odd moments such as taxi rides.

With the off-camera drama resolved, it was time to focus on the drama that the cameras would record. To Yo-Yo, this suite in particular was liberally laced with drama. In the opening moments of the film, he explains that it is his favorite of the six suites, the most spiritual and also the saddest. It's about loss, mourning, and reconciliation. The sarabande (the suite's fourth movement) has special meaning for him, since it was the final piece of music he played for his dying father.

The film bears a structural resemblance to *Falling Down Stairs*: the discussions between the artists take place at the beginning, allowing the entire performance that follows to proceed uninterrupted.

In *Struggle for Hope*, this discussion format presents a problem. Bando doesn't appear to speak English. His numerous comments and replies to Yo-Yo are in Japanese, and without subtitles it's virtually impossible to figure out what's going on. At one point, for example, viewers learn that Bando was adopted. Yo-Yo asks him what he thought about that. Bando's reply is incomprehensible.

In keeping with the artistic vision of the two principals, the suite's six movements are given special names. The prelude is named "Ritual." It begins with Yo-Yo in a pool of light, with the rest of the stage in shadow. Then Bando emerges, as a woman—a guise he maintains throughout the film. Gradually the stage becomes lighter and lighter, as Bando continually gestures toward stands of unlit candles that burst into flames in response.

In the second movement, "Mourning," Bando occupies the stage by himself and conveys the universal feeling of sadness. The movement ends with him on his knees, looking up at a circular array of candles as the rest of the stage goes into darkness.

Movement three, "Denial," returns the viewer to the opening set, with Bando clad in a light purple kimono and clutching a fan. His gestures are larger than they were in the preceding movement, Mourning, and at the conclusion he looks defiantly at the camera. This is virtually the only time during the entire performance that he acknowledges the camera's presence.

The fourth movement, "Prayer," begins with Bando huddled under a diaphanous veil in the center of the stage. He arises, removes the veil, and begins his dance. The movement ends as it began, with Bando returning to the center of the stage, falling to his knees, and pulling the veil back over his head as the lights dissolve.

"Dream," the galanterie movement (here Bach uses a folk-dance form called a gavotte), is perhaps the most interesting. Several gauze curtains are suspended throughout the stage. Bando wears a shiny golden kimono and has a small drum strapped to his chest which he plays with two small sticks. He sometimes strikes the two sticks together. Midway through the movement Yo-Yo appears onstage with his cello, but he's not playing it. Rather, he sits with his hands on his knees while Bando deftly removes the cello, carries it behind one of the curtains, then returns it as the music comes to an end.

In the final movement, "Reconciliation," Bando once again wears the same white gown as in Ritual, the first movement, though Reconciliation begins with the stage fully lighted. Yo-Yo is also onstage. At the end, the stage darkens as Bando vanishes. Yo-Yo remains briefly visible in a pool of light, then he too disappears as the camera focuses on a single, brightly burning candle in the foreground.

That ending is significant. Explaining subsequently that Bando needed a year to become fully immersed into the composition, Yo-Yo added, "It was the idea of a candle, of lighting something, and also of the flames being gradually extinguished, that was the unifying factor for him, visually and choreographically. The result was a feeling of resignation, of giving up, but of still nurturing that fire, that life in the piece."[5]

Up to this point, all the films had used Bach as a jumping-off point. Many of the films' discussions, of course, had included aspects of what made Bach such a great composer. Now it was time to let him speak for himself.

NOTES

1. Andrew L. Pincus, *Musicians with a Mission: Keeping the Classical Tradition Alive* (Boston: Northeastern University Press, 2002), p. 33.

2. Ibid.

3. Edith Eisler, "Continuity in Diversity," *Strings*, May–June 2001.

4. "Barbara Willis Sweete—Director's Notes," http://www.sonyclassical.com/releases/63203/films.html.

5. Eisler, "Continuity in Diversity."

Chapter 14

BACH—UP CLOSE
AND PERSONAL

For the visual aspect of the filming of Bach's sixth cello suite, which is written in D major, Yo-Yo chose the English Olympic-gold-medal ice dancing team, Jayne Torvill and Christopher Dean. He also chose to give primary responsibility for the narrative flow to Bach himself, as portrayed by actor Tom McCamus. McCamus as Bach appears throughout the film, reading passages that Bach wrote in his diary. Unlike the iconic images of a bewigged Bach as a sort of elder statesman of music, McCamus presents an image of Bach as a considerably younger man, in accord with the time that Bach actually composed the suites. Presumably Yo-Yo intended this device to provide some biographical context for viewers.

Johann Sebastian Bach was born in Germany in 1685 to a renowned family of musicians. He learned how to play several instruments at a young age. His life took a tragic turn at age nine when his mother died. His father followed her in death less than a year later. The orphaned 10-year-old had to live with an older brother for several years. He obtained his first job, as a church organist, when he was 18. Within a few years he had composed one of his most famous works, the organ piece *Toccata and Fugue in D Minor* (which became part of the original Walt Disney movie *Fantasia*). He married his cousin Maria Barbara in 1707.

A decade after his marriage he accepted the post of kapellmeister (the person in charge of music) at the court of Prince Leopold of Anhalt-Cöthen. The prince was a music lover and provided Bach with a small orchestra of outstanding musicians to use as he wished. Prince Leopold often joined the orchestra, as he was a skilled performer.

In Bach's previous employment, he had had to spend much of his time in duties such as rehearsing church choirs. Most such requirements were removed when he arrived at Cöthen, freeing him to devote his energies to creating music. It was one of the most prolific periods of his life. Scholars believe that the cello suites were among his first compositions following his arrival. If so, they would have marked the exact midpoint of his life—a neat bit of symbolism of which Yo-Yo must have been aware.

In 1720, his happiness was shattered when he returned from a lengthy vacation with the prince and found that his wife Maria had died in his absence. A year and a half later he married Anna Magdalena Wilcke. Between his two wives, he sired 20 children, thereby earning his nickname of "Papa Bach." To his immense sorrow, half of them died in infancy or early childhood.

Soon after Bach's wedding to Anna Magdalena, the prince married a woman who had little interest in classical music and pressured him to reduce his involvement. By that time Bach had also realized that he couldn't obtain the good education he wanted for his sons in Cöthen. So in 1723 he accepted the position of cantor of the Thomasschule in Leipzig. He remained there until his death in 1750.

By then, the emerging classical style had rendered his compositions, which were in the Baroque idiom, obsolete in the eyes of most people. Whatever fame he had was largely eclipsed by his sons Carl Philipp Emanuel and Johann Christian, who had become well known for their classical compositions. His reputation languished in relative obscurity until 1829 when Felix Mendelssohn led a performance of Bach's *St. Matthew Passion*. That performance resulted in a revival of interest in his works that has continued unabated to the present day.

There's no doubt about his stature now. Musicians who span many different styles—classical of course, plus jazz and rock 'n roll, to name just a few—incorporate him into their works. In 1977, two Voyager spacecraft blasted off and headed for deep space. On board was a golden record, which was designed to introduce life on earth to beings in other galaxies. It contained images of life on earth, brief greetings in dozens of languages, natural sounds, and a selection of 27 brief musical passages from cultures all around the globe. Three of the 27 passages were Bach's.

Yo-Yo's final film of Bach's cello suites is probably the most complex of the series of six. It is the only one, except for *Sarabande*, in which Yo-Yo has no interaction or discussions about the creative process with the artists with whom he collaborates. (In *Sarabande*, these discussions emerge organically out of the film itself, rather than standing apart from his playing.) It is also the film in which the element of polyphony is perhaps most pronounced, because the film develops several narrative and performance threads. Some of these threads continue throughout the entire film, while others appear briefly.

No less than the other five, this final film needed a central focus, a unifying element. Director Patricia Rozema, Torvill and Dean, producer Niv Fichman, composer Lesley Barber (the film is the only one that includes a separate score), and Yo-Yo agreed that this central focus would be a series of gestures—one for each movement—and the film now had its name.

Six Gestures begins with Yo-Yo, casually clad in a black shirt and sunglasses, among an immense throng of people in New York's Times Square. Titles superimposed over the scene explain what is to follow:

When Yo-Yo Ma decided to re-record
J. S. Bach's Suites for Unaccompanied Cello
He approached world champion skaters
Jayne Torvill and Christopher Dean
To join him in interpreting
The Sixth Suite

As the camera closes in on Yo-Yo, a man in a business suit asks him, "Excuse me, why Torvill and Dean?"

This is one of a number of somewhat zany touches that stylistically set the filming of Suite No. 6 in D Major apart from the others. As becomes evident later on in the film, there's also a technical factor in the way it was written that distinguishes it from its five predecessors. Most scholars believe that Bach wrote the score for a cello with five strings; the extra string allowed him to write higher notes. Players using typical four-string cellos today can encounter difficulties in matching those higher notes.

Still another difference is that the suite's format—though conforming to the customary six parts—is more free form, with a number of cadenzas and other passages that allow the cellist to demonstrate his or her virtuosity.

To Rostropovich, Suite No. 6 was the ideal finale to the set of suites. He maintained that its key of D major expressed joy and triumph, as did that most famous piece of music with similar expressions, the choral movement of Beethoven's Ninth Symphony.

In *Six Gestures*, Yo-Yo's immediate reply to the man's question of why he uses Torvill and Dean is that "I think they're extraordinary." Then he explains further, "They did for ice dancing what Bach did for the cello. Both worked with strict forms. Through working that way, they were able to find unbelievable freedom of expression, depth of expression." In other words, Bach pushed the envelope of what was regarded as possible for the cello in writing the suites. Torvill and Dean did the same thing in choreographing their routines.

The man politely thanks Yo-Yo and disappears into the crowd. Moments later Yo-Yo finds a raised stone platform, takes out a folding chair and begins to play. After a few moments, the film cuts to its first image of Bach, sitting at a table with a couple of candles and a score in front of him.

"When I came to Cöthen I was truly joyful," he begins. "I was paid quite handsomely, I had sixteen top-notch musicians, no choir [Cöthen represented his only significant period of non-religious-oriented composition], music for music's sake written at the behest of the prince my employer, an ardent young . . . friend." Immediately the camera pans to the bottom of the screen and Bach's boots, which become a visual pun: a footnote. Viewers see a print line that reads, "1. He not only loves music, he understands it."

The camera returns to the face of Bach, who adds, "And my cherished Maria Barbara with me. I intended to live here the rest of my days. At that moment I thought the world good."

That sentence segues into the prelude. In keeping with the overall theme, the film's creators have given each movement the name of a gesture. In this case, it's "Looking Upward." Throughout much of the ice dance that follows, Torvill and Dean do direct their faces upward. The camera cuts away to Yo-Yo several times, who continues to play even though hardly anyone pays attention to him.

As the second movement or allemande (entitled "Looking Inward") begins, Bach says, "Of course there are always doubts. Was I isolating myself?" That sets up a brief counterpoint with Yo-Yo, who answers the questions that Bach asks. He notes that Bach was indeed comparatively isolated because he lived his entire life within a relatively circumscribed area, unlike the far more cosmopolitan Handel.

As the scene shifts to the dancers, Dean skates briefly by himself, then approaches a bank of mirrors. Soon Torvill appears on the other side of the bank. After mirroring his movements for a while, she emerges and the two dance together. Then they head back toward the mirrors and Torvill disappears behind them, leaving behind a somewhat dazed and confused Dean.

The courante ("Hands, Feet Working") becomes very literal at several points during the dancing. Almost as an afterthought during one of his appearances, Bach mentions that he's going with five musicians to the vacation spa of Carlsbad so the prince can continue to have music whenever he wishes—the eighteenth-century equivalent of an iPod vacation.

Then viewers see a large delivery truck, with the legend "6 years, 112 works composed at Cöthen" emblazoned on its side. Up next is a brief interview with a luthier, who discusses the five-string cello. That interview dissolves into images of Yo-Yo playing his cello, superimposed on the hands of a luthier working on a cello and Bach's hands writing music. At the same time, Torvill and Dean seem to be making more elaborate hand and arm gestures than in the other movements.

The sarabande ("Hand Stroking the Face") opens with the sound of a storm in the background. Bach says, "I came home to misery. Maria Barbara was gone. She died while I was away, just . . . died."

As they dance, Torvill and Dean brush each other's faces several times. At the end Dean holds his partner's face with both hands, then slowly releases her. The two of them face each other, hands at their sides, several feet apart . . . never to reunite.

The film shifts to a car speeding through a cemetery, the camera showing dozens of ancient burial monuments; then to Bach, smoking his pipe and staring into space. "Death is my lot," he says. "Life is a symphony of sorrows."

Another footnote emphasizes the point. By the time of Maria Barbara's death, it informs us, Bach had lost his parents and all his siblings. Before Bach himself died in 1750, he had also lost 11 of his children.

The camera moves back up to the face of Bach, a devout Lutheran, who is bitter. "My God is an angry God," he says. "I know death is a release from the drudgery, I know I have to be happy for those who have left me behind, but for myself, I am not."

The gavotte ("Mannered, Courtly Gestures") begins with more bad news. "I gave Prince Leopold's life a musical score—birthdays, holidays, meetings," Bach says. "Now he is caught up with a stupid princess. She knows nothing of music, and is jealous of our friendship. Now she is the instrument he wishes to play. We have our little dance—polite, dutiful, and empty."

Torvill and Dean dance together, but without the passion they exhibited in early movements. They even clasp each other's hands while wearing white gloves.

For Bach, the emptiness cries out for a remedy. "I need a choir [one appears at once, for a moment]. My Lord and Father, I need to serve you from within the womb of my faith again. I can't have any more of these . . . dances!" And he adds that it is symbolic that one of his now-dead children was named for the prince.

The final movement ("Flight, Rebirth") allows Bach to escape from his sorrow. It begins with him saying, "And then . . . change. She has a soprano voice that is not entirely disagreeable. . . . Actually, it is lovely. She can even copy music.[1]

"She sings so finely," he continues. "And her form—Thank you, Lord, for creating a woman with such a form. It is so cold here and the miracle   •

of birth, I miss it. Warm wet little body, full of the future, full of me, full of her . . . Anna Magdelena." And he smiles.

An instant later, the screen is flooded with deep, rich color as the hands of an unseen person toss a smiling toddler into the air. Torvill and Dean make the first of numerous cameo appearances in the movement. They are now out of the confines of the darkened studio and their exuberant movements are displayed either against a blue sky with fluffy white clouds or the sides of buildings. A flight of Canada geese swoops past. Yo-Yo plays in a cathedral. A woman in a brightly colored flower-print shirt walks up to his open cello case and tosses in some money.

The meaning seems clear. Though it's likely that the suites were composed while Maria Barbara was still alive, the eruption of color and excitement at this point in the film suggests that Bach has moved beyond his personal tragedy to make music that will move people forever. It is a confirmation of Rostropovich's contention that the suite expresses joy and triumph.

Eventually Yo-Yo finishes playing the suite. By now he has attracted a crowd of several dozen passersby, many of whom take his picture as they applaud.

But the film is far from over. It cuts back to Bach, framing a slightly larger perspective in which the camera has pulled back a little to show natural light pouring in from a window in the upper right corner of the frame. "Am I wrong to find delight again? Does it make light my griefs? Do our smiles make light of death?" he asks.

No one answers. Instead, the film returns to Yo-Yo climbing down from the platform where he has been playing and putting his cello in its case. Then it quickly goes back to Bach, who says, "I did what I could, Lord. I did what I could," as a valediction.

And still the film isn't ready to wrap. In a somewhat jarring note, a woman dressed in a white lab coat comes up to Bach, who acts as if she isn't there. She explains that nearly 150 years after his death, his body was exhumed by a prominent Viennese doctor, who studied the remains and claimed that he found the evidence of Bach's musical genius.

The camera pans slowly to the right, where we see the doctor pointing to a large diagram of the human ear as he explains that the structure of Bach's ear bones explains why. . . . But the rest of his droning explanation is drowned out by an increasingly loud cello passage. The camera slowly pans back to Bach, who looks up from the manuscript he's working on, smiles, gives his head a slight shake, and returns to his task. Genius, he and Yo-Yo seem to be saying, is ultimately unknowable.

There's one final shot of Yo-Yo walking out of the frame, then Times Square gradually fades out of focus and becomes a blur. The film—and the series *Inspired by Bach*—is over.

Though the films were completed in 1997, their first appearance in the United States came the following year when they were presented in three two-hour segments on the Public Broadcasting System. Rather than presenting the suites in numerical order, PBS juggled the sequence. Perhaps because of its focus on Bach himself, *Six Gestures* came first. The others, in order, were *Falling Down Stairs* (the third suite), *Sarabande* (the fourth), *Struggle for Hope* (number five), *Water Garden* (the first), and *The Sound of the Carceri* (the second). In his review, Richard S. Ginell of *Variety* noted that the juggling "makes cinematic sense, for in this order, the films roam further afield from Bach as they unfold, becoming gradually more daring and risky in their fusion of idioms and situations."[2]

On the same day that the first two films premiered, Yo-Yo made a startling announcement during a National Public Radio broadcast. He informed listeners that he was going to abandon the cello so he could concentrate his efforts on learning to play the bandoneón. Many listeners were familiar with *Soul of the Tango*; the album's Grammy triumph just a few weeks earlier was still fresh in their minds. The news quickly became understood as a logical outgrowth of Yo-Yo's insatiable musical curiosity. But his listeners weren't happy about it. They deluged the switchboards of NPR stations across the country to register their dismay with Yo-Yo's decision.

The volume of calls forced NPR to clarify the situation. They pointed out the date of this announcement. It was April 1. Yo-Yo was simply playing a prank.

There was nothing humorous about a number of reactions to *Inspired by Bach*, some of which appeared on the same day. For the first time in his career, Yo-Yo encountered widespread criticism of what he had done.

Reviewing *Six Gestures*, Walter Goodman of the *New York Times* said, "Instead of complementing or enhancing the music or the dance, the visual antics draw attention to themselves as images dissolve and blurs come into focus. . . . 'What am I doing here?' Bach asks, and no good answer is forthcoming. Maybe that's what makes him so melancholy."[3]

Comparing the films to the companion CD that Yo-Yo released at the same time, Justin Davidson of *Newsday* said that the films were "serious, if ineffectual, attempts to discover new meanings in music. . . . The performances of the Suites on the CD 'Inspired by Bach' (an odd title, because the music was, in fact, Written by Bach) are as powerful and limpid as the films are limp."[4]

Some of the harshest words came from Yo-Yo's onetime professors at Harvard. Kirchner termed the films "baloney, unworthy of a supreme musician like Yo-Yo. I told him he should have saved a suite for Tiger Woods."[5] And Christoph Wolff, a Bach expert and the dean of the Harvard Graduate School of Arts and Sciences, said, "I found a number of things rather embarrassing in those videos."[6]

Not all judgments were so negative. *Time* magazine, for example, bestowed a mixed review, praising some films while finding others less than stellar. "But even the weaker films are fascinating for what they reveal about the processes of making interpretative art,"[7] noted Bruce Handy and Daniel S. Levy.

Variety's Ginell took a somewhat similar tack. "Some are quite imaginative, some a bit tedious, yet the best of them manage to stimulate our thoughts about Bach's power to endure even in the most alien environments," he said. "With an almost ingenuous spirit, [Yo-Yo] glides serenely through each setting, exuding a calming presence even amidst the most bizarre or fractious personalities and situations."[8]

And Wolff tempered his criticism by noting that Yo-Yo's target audience for the films wasn't professional musicians. "I think he's trying to reach out to a broad audience to whom Bach means nothing, to transmit the excitement of these pieces, by bringing in a contemporary visual dimension that he feels might really enhance the musical messages," he explained.[9]

Newsweek, however, was completely on board with what he was doing: "'Inspired by Bach' updates the suites and makes them relevant. It's easy to jaw on about timelessness, but without new music or interpretations of the old repertoire, classical music is begging for extinction."[10]

Yo-Yo would eventually earn a certain degree of validation for his efforts. *Inspired by Bach* won two Emmys and 10 Gemini awards, the Canadian equivalent to the Emmys.

And while the films technically weren't part of yet another award from another quarter, Yo-Yo could also bask in being named Billboard's 1998 Classical Artist of the Year. According to one of the publication's writers, Bradley Bambarger, "1998 saw the 43-year-old cellist at the summit of his powers and the peak of his appeal, with a series of artistically serious yet commercially momentous albums for Sony Classical."[11]

The continuing success of *Soul of the Tango*—which had been on the Billboard top-15 list for more than a year—was one factor in the acclaim from Billboard. The companion CD to *Inspired by Bach* was another. A third was the release of *The Protecting Veil* by John Tavener (who had become famous for his "Song for Athene," performed at the funeral of Princess Diana the previous year). Finally, Yo-Yo played a prominent role in recording *Music for Strings and Piano Left Hand,* featuring composers Erich Wolfgang Korngold and Franz Schmidt.

The films also provided Yo-Yo with the satisfaction of knowing that he had created something much more tangible than a concert. There was, of course, the companion CD to the recordings, which received almost universal approbation. There were the films themselves. There were the dances. And perhaps above all, there was the Toronto Music Garden.

"I'm really proud of that," he said. "It's a place where things happen because people want them to happen, and that's my paradigm for culture. I can actually go see it. It's alive. It's not ephemeral."[12]

In any event, once the films were released Yo-Yo was more than ready to move forward. By that point he was charging full steam ahead on yet another project, which he had been thinking about for some time. In an interview several years earlier, he had provided a hint of this new direction: "Do you know what I'm really interested in? How music traveled in ancient times. . . . I'm actually going to look into that. I would like to find out as much as possible."[13]

The "free-range cellist" was about to embark on his widest-ranging project to date, one that would not only traverse thousands of miles in space but also thousands of years in time.

NOTES

1. This comment about Anna Magdalena's copyist ability may be a reference to the fact that there is no authentic copy of the cello suites in Bach's own hand. The closest to an authentic copy may be one that Anna Magdalena copied, and it is not considered definitive. There are dozens of different versions extant.

2. Richard S. Ginell, "Yo-Yo Ma: Inspired by Bach Review," *Variety,* April 1, 1998.

3. Walter Goodman, "Television Review: Cellist Finds Accompanists for J. S. Bach," *New York Times,* April 1, 1998.

4. Justin Davidson, "Score One for Bach: The Music Transcends Yo-Yo Ma's New Film," *Newsday,* April 1, 1998.

5. Janet Tassel, "Yo-Yo Ma's Journeys," *Harvard Magazine,* March-April 2000.

6. Ibid.

7. Bruce Handy and Daniel S. Levy, "Yo-Yo Ma's Suite Life?" *Time,* March 23, 1998.

8. Ginell, "Yo-Yo Ma: Inspired by Bach Review."

9. Tassel, "Yo-Yo Ma's Journeys."

10. Janet Tassel, "Cross Over, Beethoven," *Newsweek*, April 20, 1998.

11. "Yo-Yo Ma has been named *Billboard*'s 'Classical Artist of the Year,'" http://www.sonyclassical.com/news/awards_top.htm.

12. Andrew L. Pincus, *Musicians with a Mission: Keeping the Classical Tradition Alive* (Boston: Northeastern University Press, 2002), p. 33.

13. Jamie James, "Yo-Yo Ma May Be a National Institution, but He Continues to Reinvent Himself," *New York Times*, December 31, 1995.

Chapter 15

DIE SEIDENSTRASSE

Early in the fourteenth century, the most famous chronicler of the world's most famous trade route began writing the most famous travel book of his era: "Here you will find all the great wonders and curiosities of Greater Armenia and Persia, of the Tartars and of India, and of many other territories."[1]

The chronicler, of course, was Marco Polo, whose account of his journey, *The Travels of Marco Polo*, was published in about 1300 A.D. Somewhat conspicuous by its absence in this brief catalog is any reference to the name of this notable trade route. There's a good reason for Polo's apparent omission. At the time he wrote his book, the route didn't have a name.

The term by which it is now known did not exist for nearly six centuries after the publication of *The Travels of Marco Polo*. Starting in 1860, German geologist and geographer Baron Ferdinand von Richthofen (who was related to the famous World War I flying ace Baron Manfred von Richthofen, the notorious "Red Baron") made the first of several expeditions to China and other Asian countries before settling down and beginning a teaching career at the University of Bonn. Von Richthofen was driven in part by the nineteenth-century European urge toward imposing Western-style order on hitherto mysterious regions of the world. These regions were now in the process of being explored and mapped. It was von Richthofen who coined the term *Die Seidenstrasse* in 1877. The Silk Road was "born."

In reality, the Silk Road had actually been "dead" for several centuries by the time von Richthofen provided it with a name. While there's no consensus about the reasons for its demise, historians generally agree that it came to an end as a viable channel of commerce about 1500 when alternate, more efficient means of trade and transportation supplanted it.

That change ended a history that traditionally dates back to the middle of the second century B.C.E., when Chinese emperor Wu sent an envoy named Zhang Qian westward in search of trading and political allies. The conquests of Alexander the Great nearly two centuries earlier had expanded the frontiers of Western influence far to the east. Therefore when Zhang Qian returned home in 115 B.C.E.—more than two decades after setting out on an extraordinarily arduous journey that would give him the sobriquet of the "Great Traveler"—people living at opposite ends of the route became dimly aware of each other's existence. In a sense, it marked the ribbon-cutting ceremony of the Silk Road.

There is, however, also a general consensus that von Richthofen's term, with its implication of a continuous thoroughfare with clearly defined beginning and ending points, is misleading. Marco Polo was one of a relative handful of people who traversed its entire length, and nearly everyone who recorded making that lengthy journey lived within a century or two of him.

For the greater part of its history, the route incorporated numerous smaller kingdoms, which jealously guarded their borders. Consequently, the trade goods destined to end up thousands of miles from their points of origin did so via a series of shorter treks, usually being loaded and unloaded several times along the way. It was common for these goods to be taxed each time, which continually raised their prices as they made their way in either direction.

The merchandise did not all follow the same route. Rather, the span of more than 5,000 miles that stretched from the eastern edge of the Mediterranean to the far coast of China was criss-crossed by dozens of disparate routes. The Silk Road could more accurately be termed the Silk Roads.

The complex route's best-known portion originated in Chang'an (modern-day Xi'an), in China. It made its way west and soon diverged into northern and southern branches to skirt the dreaded Taklamakan Desert, which was widely regarded as virtually impassable. A number of oases grew up along the two branches, which eventually converged at Kashgar after bypassing the Taklamakan. Several routes led out of Kashgar. Some continued on to the shores of the Mediterranean, while others headed south to India.

Complementary sea routes were also established. These routes began at ports in the South China Sea. After hugging the coastline for thousands of miles, the disparate roads ended up in the Red Sea. A brief overland journey delivered the cargoes to the same destinations as the land routes. By sea as by land, the goods would be transshipped repeatedly en route.

The name Silk Road is misleading in another way: Silk was far from the only product that was transported. Other luxury goods such as satin, pearls, diamonds, jade, and rubies also made their way along the route. So did more humble household items such as linen, wool, and cotton.

The travels of many of these products had profound historical consequences. One of the most important was the stirrup. When it arrived in Europe, most likely from China, it allowed horsemen not only to maintain a much firmer grip on their animals but also to gain the necessary stability to carry a long lance and shield. It therefore paved the way for the development of mounted knights—and in the eyes of some historians, the feudal system that dominated Europe for several centuries.

Another Silk Road import, gunpowder, would eventually help spell the finish to feudalism. One of the hallmarks of the feudal system was the construction of elaborate castles protected by thick stone walls. In the majority of cases these walls proved impervious to direct attacks by infantry, and also to lengthy sieges. Now these protective walls could be battered into rubble by cannons.

Not all the important imports from the Far East were destructive. First paper, and then the means of printing on paper, made their way west. After their arrival in Europe, the twin technologies allowed for the dissemination of information among a much wider portion of the population than was previously possible.

The Silk Road was definitely a two-way street. For example, knowledge of the means to manufacture glass arose in the West and made its way to China at a relatively early stage.

Just as important as the exchange of goods was the route's role as an important conduit for the exchange of ideas. The spread of major religions—Christianity, Islam, Buddhism, and others—was facilitated by the caravans. So were developments in science, such as astrology and astronomy.

The Silk Road even aided in the development of musical instruments. A Central Asian four-stringed instrument known as the *barbat* migrated west where it became known as *al oud*, the Arabic phrase for "the wood"—the material used to make the instrument. *Al oud* became part of the spread of Arabic culture into Europe that began in the eighth century. Its name became transmuted into "lute," and people who built the instrument were known as luthiers. Eventually that term would be applied to people who made any stringed instrument—such as Etienne Vatelot, who made Yo-Yo's first cello and was instrumental in the cellist's acquisition of the Davidov Strad.

The *barbat* also traveled east from Central Asia. In China it gave rise to the *pipa*, while in Japan it became the *biwa*.

Von Richthofen's newly coined term quickly caught on. The associations that it conjured up in the romantic sensibilities of the late nineteenth century were a major factor in its popularity. As author Frances Wood observes, it suggested "the timeless picture of camel trains trekking slowly along the Silk Road across deserts surrounded by snow-capped mountains, through oasis towns with bustling markets thronged with exotic inhabitants and travellers from all over northern Asia, buying and selling grapes, raisins, Hami melons, fat-tailed sheep and tough little horses."[2]

It didn't hurt this image at all that its denizens faced formidable physical obstacles during their travels. Mountains. Rivers. Bone-chilling cold. Hundred-degrees-plus heat. And not all the obstacles arose from the landscape: the wealth of the caravans attracted the attention of bandits who had to be fought off valiantly.

The names of the major cities along the route also appealed to the romantic imagination, especially since so many of them were in ruins by the nineteenth century: Baghdad. Bukhara. Kashgar. Peshawar. Samarkand. Tashkent—and many more. Even today when these once-great cities are little more than a shadow of their former selves and sit seemingly adrift in millions of square miles in countries with names that are difficult for Westerners to find on a map and pronounce—Azerbaijan, Turkmenistan, Kazakhstan, Uzbekistan, Kyrgyzstan, Tajikistan—their memories remain durable.

And despite the other cargoes that the caravans carried, in the popular imagination silk remained the crown jewel. It certainly was among the first products to travel west, and from its first appearance became associated with luxury and high living.

Another reason for silk's mystique was the air of mystery that surrounded it. According to legend, it arose more than 4,500 years ago, when a Chinese empress discovered it by accident. There is little question that it was well established by 2000 B.C.E. Its origins among the humble silkworm remained a closely guarded secret for many centuries. Eventually the secret leaked out. It was introduced in the West in the middle of the sixth century C.E. when two monks, risking torture and death if they were exposed, smuggled silkworm eggs and mulberry leaves—the insects' sole source of food—out of the Orient in their walking sticks.

Even with the cat out of the bag (or perhaps more accurately, the silkworm out of the cocoon), the Silk Road endured for another millennium. Marco Polo was a relative latecomer on the route, but his being able to make the entire journey was a historically recent development. One of the primary reasons he was able to travel the entire length was the so-called Pax Mongolia, in which the Mongol Empire—established by

Genghis Khan in the thirteenth century and expanded by his descendants to become the third-largest empire in world history—controlled most of the territory and imposed order over its far-flung regions.

Some historians believe that the decline of the Mongol Empire that began soon after reaching its apex was the primary reason for the decline of the Silk Road. Another impetus to decline may have been the emergence of new sea routes around Africa that Vasco da Gama had pioneered late in the fifteenth century. Though voyages from Asia to Europe lasted several months, they drastically lowered transportation costs and therefore the price of their cargoes. Columbus was seeking an even shorter route when he made his epochal voyage in 1492.

Of course, Yo-Yo wasn't seeking sea routes 500 years later when he became interested in the Silk Road. He joked that the original idea came when "I was in a pizza parlor. I was tired of practicing and said, 'You know, I can't play in tune. What else can I do?'"[3]

Kidding aside, he explained its actual genesis: "I've been traveling all over the world for 25 years, performing, talking to people, studying their cultures and musical instruments, and I always come away with more questions in my head than can be answered. One of these is the idea of culture as a transnational influence, and the Silk Road, though basically a trade route, also connected the cultures of the peoples who used it."[4]

The connections made by the Silk Road among cultures were so multifold that on numerous occasions, Yo-Yo has referred to the Silk Road as the "internet of antiquity." Several factors, all related to his seemingly insatiable curiosity, played pivotal roles as his idea gained momentum in his mind.

Working with O'Connor and Meyers was one such factor. The Appalachian music they played could be traced back to the British Isles and even to Scandinavia. "One of the most useful things that Mark taught me was the importance of oral traditions in which music is transmitted, but also changed, through emigration and diaspora," said Yo-Yo. "For example, eighteenth- and nineteenth-century immigrants from Anglo-Celtic lands brought their jigs, reels, and hornpipes to the New World, where successive generations of musicians transformed them into a range of different styles and repertoires."[5]

The same principles of cross-cultural transmission and change, of course, applied to other regions. Yo-Yo began zeroing in on the Silk Road during a 1994 visit to Jordan, when he traveled to the ruins of the ancient city of Petra. He was impressed by what he saw and learned that the city—which would be named one of the Seven New Wonders of the World in 2007—had been a prosperous and important trade center during the early centuries of the Silk Road.

Another formative event was a visit soon afterward to a Japanese museum. Yo-Yo was particularly fascinated by *biwas*, five-string lutes with a pear-shaped base. Some of them were decorated with scenes of musicians mounted on camels and elephants. Since neither animal was native to Japan, Yo-Yo wondered how their images had made their way there.

Yo-Yo also read a book by Theodore Levin, *The Hundred Thousand Fools of God: Musical Travels in Central Asia (and Queens, New York)*. Levin, a pianist and professor of music at Dartmouth, was an expert in the music of the central Asian region. His book was a description of how many of the musicians (the "fools of god") had fared since the 1991 breakup of the Soviet Union, which had controlled central Asia since the early 1920s. Some of them had emigrated from their homeland to Queens.

Soon afterward, Yo-Yo had an "Aha!" moment. "I had looked at lots of little pieces of information and said: aren't these interesting?" he said. "And then I asked myself whether we could start to connect all those little dots."[6]

The first step in connecting the little dots came in 1998, when Yo-Yo organized several conferences—in Boston, Paris, and Amsterdam—to discuss the feasibility of the undertaking he had begun to envision. In addition to fostering his "big picture" idea, Yo-Yo also had the opportunity to learn a new instrument. By chance, his conference in Amsterdam coincided with the recent arrival there of several Mongolian musicians. They introduced him to the *morin khuur*, a two-stringed instrument that bears a slight resemblance to a small cello. As had been the case when he saw the instruments of the Bushmen in the Kalahari, Yo-Yo wanted to play this unfamiliar device. The results were about the same as they had been in the Kalahari five years earlier.

"I can assure you having two strings doesn't make it twice as easy," he said. "When I first tried it, it was impossible to play."[7]

But he persevered, and soon grew to love the way the *morin khuur* sounded. He also felt a particular kinship with the instrument. *Morin khuur* literally means "horse-head fiddle," and the traditional carving of a horse's head at the tip of the instrument reminded him of the meaning of his last name, Ma, in Chinese.

The conferences generated enough enthusiasm in the arts world for Yo-Yo to decide to found a nonprofit organization, the Silk Road Project. He and the other conference attendees felt a sense of urgency. With the spreading worldwide influence of American pop culture and the erosive influence of other factors such as religion and politics, many of the conference participants felt that native traditions in music were rapidly disappearing. The Silk Road Project would therefore serve as a means of keeping these traditions alive and even revitalizing them. In addition, it would seek to develop new ways of understanding how music—and culture in general—circulated around the world.

There was another reason for urgency. "Every time I open a newspaper, I am reminded that we live in a world where we can no longer afford not to know our neighbors," Yo-Yo explained. "The Silk Road is a musical way to get to know our neighbors."[8]

That insight led to the organization's motto: *What Happens When Strangers Meet?* To Yo-Yo, music played a vital role in such meetings. Could he use music to improve the way that people got along? "If I know what music you love and you know what music I love, we start out having a better conversation,"[9] he said.

In undertaking such formidable objectives, the central focus would be on developing an ensemble composed of musicians from a wide variety of cultures. They would play three types of music: existing music from the Silk Road countries, new commissions, and Western music that drew on Asian influences such as Nikolai Rimsky-Korsakov's *Scheherazade* and choral music of Gustav Mahler, whose massive song cycle *Das Lied von der Erde* (*The Song of the Earth*) had been inspired by his reading of Chinese poetry.

Initial funding came from several sources. Sony Classical was one, in the expectation that the project would eventually begin recording albums. Another was the Aga Khan Trust for Culture. The Ford Motor Company also became a major sponsor.

Yo-Yo became artistic director and Levin was named executive director of the Silk Road Project. The next step was to develop the new music that would be such a vital element of the undertaking. Levin spent several months in central Asia in search of suitable composers. Chinese composer Bright Sheng returned to his native land with the same mission.

As a young man, Sheng had undergone the Cultural Revolution, whose beginnings had so alarmed Yo-Yo's father. Sheng's musical ability spared him from the arduous agricultural work that claimed many victims; he played with a band in Tibet and gained an appreciation for Chinese folk music before coming to the United States in 1982 with "no friends, no English and no money."[10]

He became acquainted with Yo-Yo when he served as page-turner for him, pianist Emanuel Ax, and violinist Yong Uck Kim during a performance in 1983. Sheng's natural composing ability soon resulted in more substantial employment; he became composer-in-residence with organizations such as the Seattle Symphony and Lyric Opera of Chicago. In 1995 he wrote *Seven Tunes Heard in China* as a solo work for Yo-Yo.

Levin and Sheng identified several dozen possible composers for the Silk Road Project, 16 of whom were eventually selected. In addition, Richard Danielpour (whose roots were Iranian), American Peter Lieberson (who had been strongly influenced by Buddhism), and Chinese classical composer Tan Dun agreed to write music for the project.

During this time, the project was also seeking musicians. In July of 2000, a disparate group of nearly 60 who spoke a variety of languages—some who flew in from their native countries, others who were already in the United States—met in Massachusetts at Tanglewood, the summer home of the Boston Symphony, to get to know each other and undertake nine intensive days of rehearsal. That winter Yo-Yo undertook a modest tour in preparation for their first real venture the following year. Stretching over a period of more than a year, this tour would incorporate a number of what could be termed minifestivals: multiday sojourns in selected cities that would encompass appearances in schools and other venues in addition to evening concerts.

Not everyone was completely sanguine about the project. "Ma has certainly traded on trust in The Project, as the Silk Roadies uniformly call it," commented one journalist. "Only a star of his stature—with management like ICM, a record label like Sony, and a circle of highly placed friends and professional associations—could have generated solid artistic momentum from such a pie-in-the-sky premise."[11]

Levin himself was cautious about the chances of success. While noting that Yo-Yo's infectious enthusiasm and optimism were vital qualities, he added, "At the same time, one does need to be aware of the harsh political realities—including all too many cultures trying to eradicate other cultures and their legacies. I am constantly hammering this home to him; it is a tough world out there."[12]

It's doubtful that Yo-Yo had similar reservations. As he explained long before the Silk Road Project was even a gleam in his eye, "Beethoven thought that through his music he could change the world. Today, rock musicians are virtually the only ones who think that."[13]

By this time, it seemed that he had mentally added the Silk Road Project to that short list. "I believe that music can act as a magnet to draw people together," he explained in the project's vision statement. "The Silk Road Project hopes to plant the seeds of new artistic and cultural growth, and to celebrate living traditions and musical voices throughout the world."[14]

NOTES

1. Marco Polo, *The Travels of Marco Polo*, translated and with an introduction by Ronald Latham (New York: Penguin Books, 1958), p. 33.

2. Frances Wood, *The Silk Road: Two Thousand Years in the Heart of Asia* (Berkeley: The University of California Press, 2002), p. 9.

3. Martin Steinberg, "Yo-Yo Ma Will Take Silk Road to China," Associated Press, September 26, 2007.

4. Edith Eisler, "Yo-Yo Ma and the Silk Road Project," *Andante* (April 2001).

5. Elizabeth ten Grotenhuis (editor), *Along the Silk Road* (Seattle, Wash.: University of Washington Press, 2002), pp. 26–27.

6. Ibid., p. 31.

7. "Interview: Cellist Yo Yo Ma on His Music and New CD," *Weekend Edition Saturday*, National Public Radio, May 25, 2002.

8. Jake Miller, "Travelers on the Silk Road: 2006," *Yoga Joyful Living* (September/October 2006).

9. Richard Covington, "Yo-Yo Ma's Other Passion," *Smithsonian Magazine* (June 2002).

10. "Bright Sheng," http://www.schirmer.com/default.aspx?TabId=2419&State_2872=2&ComposerId_2872=1436, on the G. Schirmer Associated Music Publishers Web site.

11. Ken Smith, "Setting Off on the Silk Road (Project)," *Andante* (September 2001).

12. Janet Tassel, "Yo-Yo Ma's Journeys," *Harvard Magazine* (March/April 2000).

13. David Blum, *Quintet: Five Journeys Toward Musical Fulfillment* (Ithaca, N.Y.: Cornell University Press, 1998), p. 24.

14. Yo-Yo Ma, "The Silk Road Project—Vision," http://www.silkroadproject.org/about/vision.html. Web site of the Silk Road Project, Inc.

Chapter 16

CROSSING OVER

Yo-Yo wasn't devoting all his time to the Silk Road Project. By the time it was launched, he had decided that he wanted to evoke a sound more characteristic of the Baroque era from his Strad. Part of the impetus for this new effort came from his association with O'Connor and Meyers. To keep up with them when they played as a threesome, Yo-Yo had had to change his bowing style, somewhat analogous to the way a baseball player might choke up on the bat to shorten his swing and establish more control.

Making this bowing change gave him an idea. He had never been completely comfortable playing the Strad with the numerous accoutrements that had been added over the ages, feeling that he was pushing the instrument beyond its comfort zone. "I always felt a little bad putting the Strad under all this pressure, souped up for maximum horsepower," he said. "You're always trying to find the right way to make an instrument sing."[1]

In order to make it "sing," he made several physical changes to the instrument. First he removed the end pin and gripped the cello between his legs rather than resting it on the floor.

"As I walked away from rehearsal I could imagine someone asking, 'Excuse me, are you a cowboy or a baroque cellist?'" he joked.[2]

Next he installed gut strings in place of the now-customary steel. He began using a different bow, one that would have been familiar to Bach. He flattened the bridge, the small piece of patterned wood that raises and supports the strings and increases their volume of sound.

The resulting differences in tones pleased him. He noted that the alterations provided "a much more intimate sound. By removing the innovations that over time have been made for the cello, you actually arrive at a different kind of expressivity."[3]

Early in 1999, he used the newly reconfigured Strad to collaborate with conductor Ton Koopman and the Amsterdam Baroque Orchestra—famous for their use of period instruments—in a series of concerts. Several months later this collaboration resulted in an album, *Simply Baroque*.

Bernard Holland of the *New York Times* expressed reservations about the wisdom of the move in a review of the live concerts. "Mr. Ma appeared the master of one instrument struggling splendidly to master another," he wrote. "The violin of Margaret Faultless [a member of the orchestra] and Mr. Ma's cello in 'Erbarme dich' from the St. Matthew Passion seemed to emanate not just from different rooms but different centuries as well."[4]

His *Times* colleague Michelle Dulak was considerably more harsh in her review of the album several months later, which was headlined "Dipping a Toe into the Early-Music Waters." The reference to "toe" was deliberate, suggesting a certain level of dilettantism on Yo-Yo's part, in contrast to musicians who had devoted far more time to mastering Baroque style than he had. She accused him of "slumming," a loaded term that implied that his approach was less than serious, that his foray into the realm of period instrumentation was equivalent to "just another offbeat, alternative musical culture. . . . The image that springs to mind is of the explorer among the gentle natives."[5] The last line seemed to be a clear—and clearly insulting—reference to his Kalahari trip.

All artists realize that negative reviews of their performances are an occupational hazard. To some people, however, Dulak's comments appeared to be a personal attack on Yo-Yo. Not surprisingly, Manny Ax immediately came to the aid of his friend and colleague. He was particularly incensed by Dulak's reference to slumming. "Mr. Ma's entire musical philosophy is based on exactly the opposite view: that making music in a serious way, with devotion and care, is never slumming," he wrote to the *New York Times*. "To dismiss the honest effort of a musician whose standards are as irreproachable as his playing strikes me as the height of arrogance."[6]

On the other hand, concert violinist Stephanie Chase said that while Yo-Yo had made some changes to the Strad, he hadn't "souped it down" enough. The cello still retained a number of modern touches and was therefore not authentic as a "period instrument." As a result, the album "resembles the many other crossover strategies so shamelessly promulgated by record companies and producers and falls into the category of Michael Bolton trying to sing opera arias; while Mr. Bolton is a very good pop star, he is no opera singer," she wrote. "The apparently dubious integrity of this particular venture by Mr. Ma makes its presentation under the guise of historically informed performance especially disturbing."[7]

While it may have been somewhat of a stretch to deride *Simply Baroque* as crossover music, comments such as Chase's pointed out an unavoidable fact about classical music recordings: For years, classical labels had had to deal with declining sales. Albums of even mid-level pop stars sold at many times the rate of traditional classical music. Classical labels saw the writing on the wall, and that writing said "Crossover." Bolton was a case in point. As Chase observed, no one would ever confuse him with an opera singer. Yet his 1998 release, *My Secret Passion*, shot to the top of the Billboard classical chart. Recordings by actual opera singers languished far behind.

By this time, Yo-Yo enjoyed the status of being virtually the only bankable American classical recording artist. Another 1999 release, *Solo*, was a case in point. Though the cover evoked Yo-Yo's characteristic sense of humor—it depicted him holding his cello in front of his face—the contents were of a decidedly serious nature. The music was all from twentieth-century composers. It included the Zoltán Kodály sonata that he had originally learned with the intention of playing it for the Bushmen; Bright Sheng's *Seven Tunes Heard in China*; and David Wilde's *The Cellist of Sarajevo*, which expresses the composer's feelings about the senseless sectarian violence in Bosnia. Yo-Yo's name on the cover became its primary selling point and introduced many listeners to music they probably would not have heard otherwise.

The following year he released *Simply Baroque II*, another joint effort with Koopman and the Amsterdam Baroque Orchestra. As had been the case with its predecessor, sales were brisk. Yo-Yo also joined forces again with O'Connor and Meyer, in *Appalachian Journey*. The album included several voice tracks, featuring popular singers James Taylor and Alison Krauss. It would earn Yo-Yo his 14th Grammy.

As 2000 drew to a close, *Billboard* noted that all four albums were among the top 20 in terms of sales that year. While no one was surprised by the inclusion of the two baroque albums and *Appalachian Journey*, it was a tribute to the staying power of *Solo*—and of Yo-Yo's name—that it also made the list.

The flurry that Dulak's comments had occasioned late in 1999 was nowhere in sight during Yo-Yo's activities in 2000.

Yo-Yo added yet another entry to his already bulging resume that year: television actor. He made a guest appearance on the acclaimed series *West Wing*. Playing himself in an episode centered around the White House's annual Christmas party, he performed one of the Bach suites and posed for photos with the fictional president, Josiah "Jed" Bartlet (played by Martin Sheen).

Yo-Yo was certainly no stranger to the real White House nor to real-life presidents. Of course, there had been his recognition by President Clinton in 1994 during the National Medal of the Arts ceremonies, and he had been in the White House even before that. In 1986, President Ronald Reagan invited acclaimed pianist Vladimir Horowitz, who had just been awarded the Presidential Medal of Freedom (the nation's highest award bestowed on civilians), to present a solo recital at the White House. At a reception following the recital, four members of the Marine Band orchestra began playing. During a pause, there was a rustle among the spectators. Yo-Yo and Itzhak Perlman, who were among the guests, emerged to replace two of the players and perform the first movement of Mozart's *Eine Kleine Nachtmusik*.

"It was an impromptu decision," Yo-Yo said. "Too bad I didn't have time to get a red jacket [referring to the formal playing apparel of the Marines]."[8]

There was nothing impromptu about Yo-Yo's appearance the following year when President Reagan hosted a private dinner for Crown Prince Akihito and Crown Princess Michiko of Japan. The president asked Yo-Yo to perform a solo recital following the dinner.

A decade later, President Clinton invited him to a state dinner for Chinese president Jiang Zemin. Five years further on, in 2002, Yo-Yo was one of eight people to be awarded the National Medal of the Arts by President George W. Bush. As part of the ceremony, Yo-Yo performed a duet with National Security Advisor Condoleezza Rice, herself a classically trained pianist. And three years later Yo-Yo and his wife were on the guest list as President Bush hosted a dinner honoring Prince Charles and his wife Camilla.

Yo-Yo capped 2000 with the recognition of a remarkable milestone. He and Ax gave a recital in December at Avery Fisher Hall to mark the 25th anniversary of their collaboration. "An unbroken current of empathetic understanding seems to flow back and forth between them, allowing an extraordinary degree of freedom and spontaneity," noted Edith Eisler in her review of the concert. "Clearly, they know that they have created something special, and Ma, with wonderfully humble sincerity, thanked Ax for 25 years of musical partnership and personal friendship."[9]

However heartfelt the appreciation that showered down on Yo-Yo and Ax, concerts such as this one were limited to a relative handful of spectators. In March the following year, a worldwide television audience in the hundreds of millions saw Yo-Yo and Perlman perform excerpts from the five film scores nominated in the category of Best Original Score at the Academy Awards. Yo-Yo had more than a passing interest in the outcome.

Tan Dun's music for *Crouching Tiger, Hidden Dragons* was one of the five nominees, and Yo-Yo had been featured on the soundtrack. So he must have been delighted when it received the Oscar—one of four that the film garnered, including the prestigious Best Foreign Language Film. At a reception afterward, he and Perlman posed for cameramen in front of a giant-sized Oscar statue. It didn't take long for the two of them to begin cutting up, allowing the public a view of the sense of humor they shared just as much as they shared a world-class level of talent.

An even larger audience saw Yo-Yo in early February of 2002 when he participated in perhaps his greatest-ever crossover: the opening ceremonies of the Winter Olympics in Salt Lake City, Utah. More than 50,000 people jammed Rice-Eccles Stadium on the University of Utah campus, while according to estimates three and a half billion people—more than half of the world's population—watched on television. Yo-Yo and pop music superstar Sting played Sting's 1980s hit single, "Fragile," while sitting on a giant replica of an ice hockey puck in the center of the stadium ice rink. The Mormon Tabernacle Choir and the Utah Symphony Orchestra provided instrumental and vocal support for the two men.

Sting pointed out that the selection was especially appropriate, coming so soon after the terrorist attacks on the World Trade Center in New York City and the Pentagon in Washington, D.C., that claimed the lives of thousands of people on September 11, 2001. Yo-Yo had been deeply affected by the tragedy, especially since it was followed a few days later by the death at age 81 of renowned classical violinist Isaac Stern. From the moment Stern heard Yo-Yo play in Paris at the age of five, he had taken an interest in his career. In particular, he guided Yo-Yo to Leonard Rose, who had had such a profound effect on Yo-Yo's development. When Yo-Yo achieved the stardom that Stern had predicted, the two of them performed frequently together and collaborated on several notable recordings. His passing closed a chapter in Yo-Yo's life.

On September 30, 2001, Yo-Yo joined opera soprano Leontyne Price as a featured performer in a Concert of Remembrance for the 9/11 victims at Carnegie Hall. He had been in Chicago for several days prior to the concert, playing the premiere of the Cello Concerto by Elliott Carter— yet another new work for which Yo-Yo was the inspiration. He flew back immediately afterward to perform that afternoon at Stern's private funeral service in Connecticut, then returned to New York for the evening concert. He began his portion of the program with "Appalachia Waltz," the folk-inspired piece he had recorded with Mark O'Connor and Edgar Meyer, then played Bach's Cello Suite No. 5 in C Minor. "If you are looking for something to depend on at this time of loss and confusion, Yo-Yo Ma playing the Bach cello suites will do just fine,"[10] said critic Anthony Tommasini.

A month later, he joined several other notable musicians in a farewell public concert for Stern at Carnegie Hall. Yo-Yo's participation was particularly fitting. Among his many noteworthy contributions to music, Stern had spearheaded the effort to save Carnegie Hall in 1960—thereby allowing the building to serve as the focal point for Hiao-Tsiun Ma's dream for his son shortly thereafter.

In view of these moving experiences, Yo-Yo could certainly concur with Sting's explanation of his choice of "Fragile" to help open the Olympics: "It's a song about violence and the fragility of life in the face of terrorism, guns and bullets. We are fragile beings."[11]

The song was appropriate in other ways. Dick Ebersol, chairman of NBS Sports, noted that the opening ceremonies convey "the impression, even for a brief moment, that we can all get along."[12]

Because of the association of doves with getting along—with peace—organizers wanted to incorporate a flight of the birds. Doves, however, were also "fragile beings." A night release could have disoriented the birds, preventing them from returning to their cages and perhaps becoming prey for predators as they circled in confusion. In their stead, more than a dozen skaters swirled around Sting and Yo-Yo in the midst of their performance, each one trailing a cloth kite in the shape of a dove.

There were even more "fragile beings" involved in the opening ceremonies: the musical instruments that belonged to Yo-Yo and the members of the orchestra. They simply wouldn't do well in temperatures in the 20s. The frigid conditions could damage the wood, and the strings could easily fall out of tune. There was no way that Yo-Yo was going to risk his precious instruments in live performance in these conditions. Nor would any of the Utah Symphony musicians.

That created a dilemma. As Ebersol's words suggested, the opening ceremonies would set the tone for the rest of the Games. In turn, Don Mischer, the executive producer of the opening ceremonies, explained, "Music is more or less the soul of the ceremonies."[13] Central to the expression of this soul was the quality of the sound. But the frigid conditions ruled out the use of first-rate musical instruments. There was another consideration. Musicians' fingers would quickly turn numb in the below-freezing temperatures, denying them the precise control they would require to produce superb sound.

A solution was readily at hand. Well before the Olympics opened, the musicians, including Yo-Yo, would record the music in a studio using their customary instruments. On the night of the ceremonies, the musicians would play the music. However, the music that the stadium and television audiences would hear—unless they were seated right next to the musicians—was the recording. To avoid risking their own instruments, the musicians were provided with relatively inexpensive instruments to use during the performance. When the Olympics were over, the instruments were donated to local schools.

David Green, the Utah Symphony's orchestra manager, found it somewhat disorienting to sit in the midst of the musicians and hear them playing while their prerecorded track boomed throughout the stadium. Some instruments stood out, while others were barely audible. "It was like an orchestra that wasn't well-balanced," he said. "I think the world would have looked at the Utah Symphony pretty sadly."[14]

The musicians, however, enjoyed themselves. Ryan Selberg, a cellist in the orchestra, said, "Even though we were playing to the pre-recorded tracks, it was quite a thrill to play some of the exciting music (especially the new John Williams piece, Call of the Champions) and feel the excitement and energy of the crowd!"[15]

He added, "Yo-Yo was there, too! His contributions in the song with Sting were beautiful, very free and jazz-like counterpoint."[16]

As was the case with the other musicians, Yo-Yo wasn't faking it. He *was* playing "Fragile." But he was playing it on an instrument that had recently been built by a local luthier, using his Montagnana as a model. And what the audience really was hearing had been recorded in the warmth and security of a recording studio weeks earlier.

When the performance was finished, Yo-Yo was his usual ebullient—and spontaneous—self. He and Sting left the stage waving to the chorus and orchestra and blowing kisses to them. The audience returned the favor, giving a thundering ovation for their performance.

Yo-Yo's mood was considerably more somber later that year. On September 11, 2002, the first anniversary of the 9/11 attacks, Yo-Yo became the first musician of any type to appear at Ground Zero. He played music from the Bach cello suites—in particular, the sarabande from the fifth suite, the same music he'd played at his dying father's bedside and at Carnegie Hall in the Concert for Remembrance—as former New York City Mayor Rudy Giuliani read the names of the victims.

But in spite of the somberness, Yo-Yo could take heart from one thing. The Silk Road Project had achieved liftoff. In fact, it had soared into orbit.

NOTES

1. James Oestreich, "Making a 1712 Cello Sound Less Modern," *New York Times,* February 20, 1999.

2. Toby Faber, *Stradivari's Genius: Five Violins, One Cello, and Three Centuries of Enduring Perfection* (New York: Random House, 2004), p. 202.

3. Ibid.

4. Bernard Holland, "Music Review; Yo-Yo Ma Looks Back, With His Cello," *New York Times,* February 23, 1999.

5. Michelle Dulak, "Dipping a Toe Into the Early-Music Waters," *New York Times,* August 1, 1999.

6. Emanuel Ax, "Yo-Yo Ma: Far From Charity," *New York Times,* August 15, 1999.

7. Stephanie Chase, "Yo-Yo Ma: A 'Retrofitted' Cello," *New York Times,* September 5, 1999.

8. Harold C. Schonberg, "In the East Room, Horowitz and 2 Surprises," *New York Times,* October 6, 1986.

9. Edith Eisler, "A Dynamic Duo on Their Silver Anniversary," *Andante* (March 2001).

10. Anthony Tommasini, "Music Review: A Concert Offers City Some Time For Healing," *New York Times,* October 1, 2001.

11. Alan Abrahamson, "Winter Olympics: It's Quite a Balancing Act. Ceremony: Sept. 11 Changed Things, but Organizers Went For, and Got, a Mixture of History, Tradition and Emotion," *Los Angeles Times,* February 9, 2002.

12. Ibid.

13. Christopher Reynolds, "Winter Olympics: The Music Isn't Live, Either. Cold Weather and a Global Audience Require Performers to Try to Match Recordings during the Opening and Closing Ceremonies," *Los Angeles Times,* February 23, 2002.

14. Ibid.

15. Ryan Selberg, *Internet Cello Society Newsletter,* March/April 2002, http://cello.org/Newsletter/marapr02.htm.

16. Ibid.

Chapter 17

GETTING UP TO SPEED ON THE SILK ROAD

It is ironic that the Silk Road Ensemble began its initial tour in Germany on August 19, 2001—just over three weeks before the jetliners hijacked by al-Qaeda terrorists began crashing into their targets in the United States. If anything, the September 11 atrocity seemed to underscore the objectives of the Silk Road Project.

"There is an unbelievable need for people to come together at this time," Yo-Yo said a few weeks after the September 11 tragedy. "There is an incredible power in music and this is a unique time to make a difference culturally."[1]

The September 11 attack definitely had an influence on the group's itinerary. They had originally been scheduled to go to Tajikistan and Kazakhstan in the fall. When the war in nearby Afghanistan soon followed the attacks, the region became too dangerous for travel.

Undaunted, the group continued to tour at a time when many people were afraid to fly. They made several stops in Europe and Japan before coming to the United States.

Seattle, Washington, was the logical choice to be the first American venue for the Silk Road Ensemble. Yo-Yo was familiar with it as a performer, the city has a large Asian American population, and it is one of the chief American ports exporting to Asia. The critical reaction to the Silk Road Ensemble there was typical of the group's reception everywhere.

"From the opening notes of Sunday's first of five Benaroya concerts, it was clear that the project reflects the kind of quality you'd expect of artistic director and cellist Yo-Yo Ma: only the best," commented *Seattle*

Times music critic Melinda Bargreen. "All of it was astonishing: music to stimulate the ear and the imagination, music to take you outside your ordinary life and move you halfway around the world."[2]

The group was still touring when their first album, *Silk Road Journeys: When Strangers Meet*, was released. "We had an amazing mix of instruments, and people just figured out what to play and where to fill in," Yo-Yo said. "I think that's the way people have always made music."[3]

Chris Nickson of *All Music Guide* noted that "It's both ambitious and daring, two qualities that have been trademarks of Yo-Yo Ma's career. . . . The instruments, from Wu Man's pipa to Joel Fan's piano, work together, whether on traditional or commissioned material, to create something that's challenging to both listeners and performers and offers a strong impression of the journeys of the past."[4]

The tour concluded in the early summer of 2002 in Washington, D.C., at the Smithsonian Folklife Festival. For the first time in its history, the festival had a single theme: "The Silk Road: Connecting Cultures, Creating Trust." Organizers sought to provide a mini-Silk Road experience for hundreds of thousands of festival goers. A multitude of musicians, artisans, and cooks offered food, music, and demonstrations of such Silk Road crafts as calligraphy, carpet weaving, glassblowing, and more.

The following year, the Barbash family became involved with Yo-Yo once again. They had enjoyed their experience with their commission so much that they decided to celebrate their 50th anniversary by commissioning a work for Yo-Yo's good friend Manny Ax. Then they had another idea: a double concerto for Yo-Yo and Ax to honor the 25th anniversary of their playing together.

Since Yo-Yo was so thoroughly involved in the Silk Road Project by then, he suggested Bright Sheng as the composer. In keeping with the spirit of the Silk Road, Sheng added two Chinese solo instruments in the *Song and Dance of Tears*, the title of the work. One was the pipa, an instrument similar to the lute. The other, the sheng, a mouth organ, is one of the oldest musical instruments in the world. Dating back 1,000 years before the birth of Christ, it consists of more than a dozen pipes up to two feet long that are inserted into a brass bowl with a short mouthpiece.

The work premiered in March, 2003. The New York Philharmonic played all three Barbash commissions in a single evening, which likely set some sort of informal world record.

Once again the Barbashes had a winner. "Bright Sheng merges the silvery, tremulous plucking of the pipa, a Chinese lute, and the reedy hum and blast of the sheng, a mouth organ, with Ma's mellifluous cello and the staunchly Western sound of the piano," Justin Davidson of *Newsday* commented. "Pulling these sonic fusions off is technically tricky . . . but Sheng has a brilliant ear for sound."[5]

Allan Kozinn of the *New York Times* added, "The New York Philharmonic could take what ought to be its rightful place as a vital contributor to the growth of this country's musical culture if it regularly presented programs like the one it played on Wednesday evening."[6]

Not long afterward, Yo-Yo released the result of yet another global jaunt. This time he went back to Latin America, where he musically crossed the border from Astor Piazzolla's Argentina to Brazil. The border crossing was more than metaphorical as the resulting album—*Obrigado Brazil*—was very different from *Soul of the Tango*. Rather than focusing on a single composer and a single dance, Yo-Yo chose to explore the entire spectrum of Brazilian rhythmic styles. Though his approach to the music was different from *Soul of the Tango*, it brought a similar result from the musical world: Early the following year, *Obrigado Brazil* notched his 15th Grammy. As had been the case with his two most recent award-winning albums—*Soul of the Tango* and *Appalachian Journey*—the Grammy was in the Best Classical Crossover category.

The award also highlighted a situation that led journalist John Fleming to ask rhetorically later that year: "Yo-Yo Ma is the biggest name in classical music. So why does he make so few classical recordings these days?"[7]

By that time he had released *Yo-Yo Ma Plays Ennio Morricone*, an album in which he collaborated with the noted Italian composer. Though Morricone—born in 1928—had been trained in the classical tradition, he became best known for writing more than 500 film scores. He put himself on the map in the mid-1960s when he worked with director Sergio Leone on the so-called "spaghetti westerns" such as *A Fistful of Dollars*, *For a Few Dollars More*, and *The Good, the Bad and the Ugly*. The films catapulted actor Clint Eastwood to stardom; more than four decades later, Eastwood would present Morricone with a Lifetime Achievement Award at the 2007 Academy Awards. (Ironically, Morricone never won an Oscar for any individual score even though he was nominated five times.) Morricone also composed the scores for *The Untouchables*, *The Mission*, *Once Upon a Time in America*, and *Cinema Paradiso*.

As if the album with Morricone were not achievement enough, Yo-Yo also recorded *Obrigado Brazil: Live in Concert*, a sequel to his Grammy winner. As critic Jonathan Widran noted, "The legendary cellist struck an incredible crossover chord with 2003's lush, exotic excursion *Obrigado Brazil*, which was the fastest-selling recording of his career. . . . Inspired by working in the studio with clarinetist Paquito D'Rivera, guitarists Sergio and Odair Assad, singer/guitarist Rosa Passos, pianist Kathryn Stott, percussionist Cyro Batista, and bassist Nilson Matta, Ma gathered the group for an electrifying live show at Carnegie Hall—which is the basis for this compelling multicultural concert disc."[8] While some people groused that the album title was misleading—it included several of Piazzolla's works in additional to Brazilian music—record buyers weren't deterred.

Having recorded most of the music in the standard cello repertoire early in his career, Yo-Yo had become increasingly reluctant to repeat it. The one notable exception was the Bach suites. Even that he had repeated with a twist, in the form of the *Inspired by Bach* films.

His sole new classical release in 2003 had been *Paris: La Belle Epoque*, with pianist Kathryn Stott, featuring music by European composers Gabriel Fauré, César Franck, Jules Massenet, and Camille Saint-Saëns. In 2004, he reunited with conductor Ton Koopman and the Amsterdam Baroque Orchestra for *Vivaldi's Cello*—and as the mini-brouhaha several years before had suggested, even that was suspect in some circles as "classical" music because he played the modified Strad.

Yo-Yo's distaste for repetition had helped impel his musical experimentation. Many people admired Yo-Yo for championing contemporary music in his recordings. In 2002, for example, he contributed to composer Philip Glass's soundtrack for the film *Naqoyqatsi* and released *Yo-Yo Ma Plays John Williams*, featuring the 1994 concerto and several of Williams' other classical works. However, these albums didn't sell especially well.

"So, crossover material increasingly dominates Ma's catalog,"[9] John Fleming continued in his 2004 critique, adding that Yo-Yo was fortunate to even have a catalog in an era when classical labels were jettisoning a number of artists. He further noted that Sony Classical, as was the case with other companies, was reissuing earlier performances of various artists. Not surprisingly, a number of these reissues included Yo-Yo. Because many of these reissues sold at reduced prices, Fleming concluded, "Old music at a discount. Somehow, that sums up the problem with the classical recording business."[10]

The classical music market may have been depressed. No one would ever say the same thing about Yo-Yo. His ebullience and enthusiasm had been on display in May that year when he returned to his alma mater to receive the Harvard Arts Medal from fellow alumnus John Lithgow. Hundreds of students and faculty members packed Sanders Theater for a nearly hour-long discussion between the two men, followed by a recital by Yo-Yo.

During the discussion, he made an astonishing admission. He explained that because he had started playing the cello at such a young age, he never made a conscious decision to make a career of music. The catalyst for making that decision his own came during his early 30s when a friend told him that he needed to stop acting as if touring was an interruption of his life. At that time Yo-Yo had already received the Avery Fisher Prize, acquired two very expensive cellos, become a successful recording artist with several Grammys, and appeared on *Mister Rogers' Neighborhood*, to itemize only a partial list of his career achievements.

In essence, Yo-Yo told Lithgow, at that point he'd been a musician for more than two decades and still wasn't sure if it was what he really wanted to do. As a result, he went through a self-examination that convinced him that music would allow him to explore life and the world around him—the same goal that had sent him to Harvard so many years earlier and ignited his love of learning. At that point, he said, "I was able to say, okay, I do have a passion, this is something I can readily sign on to do."[11]

During that same discussion, Yo-Yo also touched on the downside of fame. Calculating that he had spent nearly 20 of the past 30 years on the road—which he underscored by recounting to the audience that during the previous week he'd flown to Europe, conducted a four-city tour with Koopman and the Amsterdam Baroque Orchestra, and returned home—he observed that nothing was harder than being away from home and family.

"You miss the first steps, you miss the first words, whatever. It's gone forever,"[12] he told Lithgow and the audience.

After the Harvard ceremony, Yo-Yo continued to advance the Silk Road Project's goals. In addition to ongoing concerts—in 2003 the ensemble made the trip to central Asia that had been postponed by the 9/11 attacks—he began expanding the concept of residencies at various institutions. For example, he joined forces with the Peabody Essex Museum in Salem, Massachusetts, in the autumn of 2004. The event comprised workshops for youngsters, exhibitions of Asian art, storytelling, and even a commission for a musical work that became part of several subsequent concerts at the museum.

In 2005, Yo-Yo launched an annual fall festival with Harvard as part of a five-year collaboration with the university. During a week-long residency, ensemble members would interact with Harvard students and faculty in intensive discussions of Silk Road-related matters and musical performances. That same year marked the release of the second Silk Road album, *Silk Road Journeys: Beyond the Horizon*. And early in 2006, several ensemble members served as artists in residence at the Rhode Island School of Design, where they created a number of new compositions.

In mid-May that year, Yo-Yo made a journey that by now was starting to seem almost routine in terms of the thousands of miles that it encompassed. He flew from Azerbaijan to Tel Aviv, Israel, where he spent four days before flying to Italy. His next stop was a brief visit in Japan before returning to the United States.

There was nothing routine about Yo-Yo's reason for visiting Tel Aviv. He had just been named as one of three recipients of the Dan David Prize. This prize honors outstanding achievements in science, technology, and culture, and is awarded in three categories: past time, present time, and future time. Yo-Yo was honored in the past time category, for his contributions in protecting cultural heritages. The prize was accompanied by $1 million, by far the largest amount of money he had ever been awarded.

"This is like the sky falling down,"[13] he told journalists in Tel Aviv, describing his reaction when he learned of the honor a short time earlier.

The money came at an opportune moment. The Silk Road Ensemble was on the verge of launching its most ambitious project, a year-long residency in Chicago with more than 250 events in a variety of disciplines. The sudden windfall would help provide financial underpinning.

Yo-Yo had several reasons for choosing to locate the residency in the Windy City. One reason was practical: more than 100 million people—a third of the population of the United States—lived within 500 miles of the city. Another reason was that Chicago had a long tradition of hosting major international events such as the 1893 World's Fair. Finally, its network of sister cities included Amman, a city in the Middle East nation of Jordan and the site of Yo-Yo's 1994 visit that perhaps more than anything else inspired the Silk Road Project. Standing at one end of the Silk Road and gazing in awe at the ruins of Petra, he had realized that his ancestral homeland of China lay at the other end.

Silk Road Chicago began officially on June 26, 2006. More than 13,000 people packed the city's Millennium Park for a free concert given by the Silk Road Ensemble. Yo-Yo introduced several of the works with brief explanations of their historical and cultural significance. The throng expressed its appreciation via a standing ovation when the concert was completed. Yo-Yo and the ensemble expressed their appreciation for the applause by performing two encores.

Dozens of community organizations became involved with scores of events in succeeding months. Ensemble musicians offered master classes and visited schools. The Chicago Symphony Orchestra devoted much of its programming to music connected with the Silk Road. The Art Institute of Chicago, one of the nation's leading art museums, mounted a show called *Beyond the Silk Road: Travel, Trade, and Transformation*. It was one of the largest exhibitions the museum had ever put together.

Yo-Yo still had energy for concerts elsewhere and for recording. In January of 2007, he released *Appassionato,* with 11 tracks that spanned the breadth of his recording career and included four new ones. As the title suggested, it was music that Yo-Yo felt particularly strongly about. Most of it was of a romantic nature, and the timing of the release made the album what many people termed "the perfect Valentine's Day gift."

This timing may have been one of the primary reasons why the album debuted in the top spot on the *Billboard* classical chart. It would soon rise to number 79 on the Billboard 200, which ranks sales of recordings in all genres. That ranking was the highest position that any of Yo-Yo's albums had ever reached.

In June, Silk Road Chicago ended with the "Stone Horse Project," a story about a magical piece of silk made by a peasant woman. The wind snatches it away from her and her sons set out to recover it, overcoming dangers along the way. The music featured Yo-Yo, the Silk Road Ensemble, the Chicago Symphony Orchestra, and hundreds of schoolchildren who played a variety of instruments that included drums, rattles, bongos, and even bubble wrap.

To prepare the youngsters for their participation, Yo-Yo visited their schools. One was the Finkl Academy, where principal Susan Jensen said, "I wasn't sure any of them would know who he was, so I told them, 'What Sammy Sosa is to baseball, Yo Yo Ma is to music.' Then one astute fourth-grader looked at him and said, 'But you're not Sammy Sosa!' And Yo Yo looked right back at him and said, 'No, but I have very good pitch.'"[14]

Adults might have groaned at the pun. Not the kids. Jensen continued, "He had them eating out of his hand after that."[15]

Shortly afterward, Yo-Yo released *New Impossibilities.* The album's tracks were recorded during a series of concerts with the Chicago Symphony Orchestra. The title of the album came from Mark Twain's book *Life on the Mississippi,* in which he referred to Chicago as a city that was always changing, a place of "new impossibilities."

The album debuted at the top spot on the Billboard classical chart when it was released in August. Critical commentary was nearly all positive. "Yo-Yo Ma has pulled an ace from his sleeve with his most recent album *New Impossibilities,*" noted Roberto Perez-Franco. "Far from canonical, the pieces on the record are wild, living, breathing music."[16] He did express a few reservations. "'The Galloping Horses,' albeit interesting, struck me as too shallow to be taken seriously, evoking images closer to playful hamsters than running stallions."[17]

Silk Road Chicago ended, but for Yo-Yo—the "friendly horse"—life would continue at a full gallop.

NOTES

1. "The Silk Road Project Adds Concerts in Dallas and Atlanta," http://www.silkroadproject.org/press/releases/011010.html.

2. Melinda Bargreen, "The Silk Road Project: It's Smooth, Heavenly and Engaging," *Seattle Times*, May 14, 2002.

3. Jake Miller, "Travelers on the Silk Road: 2006," *Yoga + Joyful Living* (September-October 2006).

4. Chris Nickson, *Silk Road Journeys: When Strangers Meet,* All Music Guide, http://www.billboard.com/bbcom/discography/more.jsp?tp=albums&pid=9122&aid=531035.

5. "Bright Sheng—The Song and Dance of Tears," http://www.schirmer.com/Default.aspx?TabId=2420&State_2874=2&workId_2874=32935, on the Web site of G. Schirmer Associated Music Publishers, Inc.

6. Allan Kozinn, "Music Review: A Program Angry, Lyrical and Wacky," *New York Times*, March 8, 2003.

7. John Fleming, "Selling Yo-Yo Ma to the Masses," *St. Petersburg Times*, October 31, 2004.

8. Jonathan Widran, "Obrigado Brazil—Live in Concert: Critic's Review," All Music Guide, http://music.msn.com/album/?album=32405621&menu=review.

9. Fleming, "Selling Yo-Yo Ma to the Masses."

10. Ibid.

11. "Arts First: An Evening with Yo-Yo Ma," http://athome.harvard.edu/dh/yym.html. "The mission of Harvard@Home is to provide the Harvard community and the broader public with opportunities for rich in-depth exploration of a wealth of topics through Web-based video programs of the highest caliber" (quotation from the home page of the Web site, June 6, 2007).

12. Ibid.

13. Nathan Burstein, "Following the Silk Road to Tel Aviv," *Jerusalem Post*, May 24, 2006.

14. "Silk Road Chicago Ends with Collaborative Fable Featuring Yo-Yo Ma and School Children," *International Herald Tribune*, June 1, 2007.

15. Ibid.

16. Roberto Perez-Franco, "CD Review: An Experiment in Musical, Cultural Fusion—Yo-Yo Ma's Latest CD Tells the Story of Asia's Silk Road," *The Tech*, November 30, 2007.

17. Ibid.

Chapter 18

THE BEAT GOES ON...
AND ON...AND ON

It is the evening of Saturday, September 15, 2007. The Seattle Symphony is opening its season, and Yo-Yo is the headliner, almost exactly six months after his March 12 appearance in the city with the Silk Road Ensemble.

This time the music is far more traditional, and as had been the case in March, the concert has been a sellout for months. When a few unused tickets trickle back, the box office resells them for half their original cost. In addition, the symphony is leveraging Yo-Yo's presence for a postconcert gala with ticket prices starting at $450 per person. The fete includes a preconcert cocktail reception, champagne at intermission, a postconcert dinner with dancing—and the chance to meet Yo-Yo in person. For many of the symphony's well-heeled patrons, the chance to press the flesh of the greatest superstar of classical music is well worth the money. They snap up gala tickets by the hundreds.

Yo-Yo's popularity and prestige in Seattle go back nearly 35 years to his first visit in October 1972.

"I almost started my playing life with the Seattle Symphony, in their 'Stars of the Future' series," he recalled. "It was right after my freshman week in college, and I told my roommate, 'I've got to go away for a week.' He just looked at me."[1]

Reviewing the concert, *Seattle Post-Intelligencer* music critic Rolf Stromberg wrote, "Yesterday afternoon a Seattle audience was treated to a momentous occasion when 16-year-old Yo-Yo Ma played Antonin Dvořák's

Concerto for Cello and Orchestra in B-minor, Opus 104, at the Opera House. It was exciting, indeed.

"All in all this intense young man is a cellist to watch. He knows his instrument to the ultimate and thus can exploit the flourishes of the Dvořák to the fullest. The audience yesterday gave him a standing ovation. He deserved nothing less."[2]

Seattle has indeed watched Yo-Yo ever since then. When he brought the Silk Road ensemble here in 2002, all five evenings were sellouts. *Seattle Times* music critic Melinda Bargreen wrote, "Seattle music lovers continued their Silk Road journey to strange and wonderful places Monday evening, when Yo-Yo Ma sprinted onstage with his cello as if en route to a particularly promising adventure. That proved to be the case, happily for the capacity audience (and the 200 extra listeners who packed an added downstage seating area)."[3]

Perhaps because of Yo-Yo's guaranteed star power, Seattle Symphony music director Gerard Schwarz can depart from the traditional concert format. While there are obviously many exceptions, this traditional format normally contains three works. It begins with a relatively short composition, often upbeat in nature. That is typically followed by a concerto that shows off the ability of the visiting soloist. Following intermission, another long piece—most often a symphony—concludes the program.

Tonight's program features six compositions rather than the usual three, so in a sense it is actually a pair of mini-concerts. It opens with George Gershwin's *An American in Paris*, followed by Yo-Yo as soloist in Gabriel Fauré's *Elégie* for Cello and Orchestra, with Maurice Ravel's *Daphnis and Chloe Suite No. 2* rounding out the first half. Ravel's *Pavane for a Dead Princess* opens the second half. Yo-Yo plays Camille Saint-Saëns' Cello Concerto No. 1, a staple of the cello literature. Ravel's rousing *Bolero* will bring the evening to a close.

Clearly, the theme and focal point is the city of Paris. Fauré, Ravel, and Saint-Saëns all lived there, while Gershwin and Yo-Yo also had strong connections to the city. In a neat bit of symmetry, the latter two came to Paris from almost diametrically opposite directions, Gershwin from the United States and Yo-Yo (via his parents) from China.

Opening with the Gershwin composition is sure to prime the audience for an enjoyable evening. Gershwin sought to evoke the exuberant atmosphere of Paris, especially for visiting Americans during the heyday of the 1920s. A characteristic sonic feature of the City of Light was its taxi horns, and Gershwin not only wrote their distinctive sound into his composition but even bought some horns to take back to the United States so as to insure complete authenticity in performances when he returned home.

As the applause dies down when the Gershwin is finished, there is an expectant hush, for the audience awaits Yo-Yo's appearance. From the moment that the stage door opens and he walks onstage with Schwarz behind him, it is plain that the audience is amped up for Yo-Yo. The applause is long and heartfelt. He smiles and bows, busses concertmistress Ani Kavafian (whom he has known since the 1980s), then appears to share a joke with the cellists.

Moments later he shifts gears and immediately gets into character as Schwarz begins the Fauré *Elégie*. For much of its 10-minute length as he communes with the music, Yo-Yo's eyes are closed. At one point he appears to be briefly saying something to himself. Several times he gently rocks his cello. During a particularly passionate part, his mouth flies wide open. When it ends, the applause quickly builds, then dies out almost as rapidly. It is definitely not as enthusiastic as it had been when he walked out on stage. Perhaps this is a natural response to the nature of the music, which is somber and reflective rather than rousing.

Nevertheless, it is apparent that he has touched at least some members of the audience. "So gorgeous," one woman whispers reverently to her companion as they head for the lobby.

The somber mood continues when the orchestra plays Ravel's funereal *Pavane* after intermission. The mood changes as soon as Yo-Yo begins playing the Saint-Saëns, an active 20-minute piece. It has few respites for its solo cellist. During those brief interludes, he remains involved in the music, looking at the nearby musicians and smiling at them.

While he is playing, the hush that falls over the house is almost palpable. Just a few weeks shy of his 52nd birthday, Yo-Yo still has an unlined face, so every expression is plainly visible. Sometimes he smiles, sometimes he frowns, sometimes he talks to himself. Throughout the piece, he continually changes his position in relation to his cello. Sometimes he leans over it, so close that he could almost kiss it. At others he leans back and his movements become more expansive. Once he almost rises out of his chair.

When the final notes fade away, the audience is quickly on its feet. This time the response is loud, long, enthusiastic, and sustained. Yo-Yo basks in the applause, kisses concertmistress Kavafian several times, exchanges low fives with several violinists, and pats a double bass player on the shoulder before exiting the stage.

Moments later he is back, and when he gestures to Kavafian, the audience reaction is almost delirious: there will be an encore. Yo-Yo's longstanding rapport with Kafavian is obvious as she rises to her feet. She looks almost like an old-time hoedown fiddler as she bobs and weaves around the seated Yo-Yo. Much of their playing—of a movement from

Maurice Ravel's Sonata for Violin and Cello—consists of plucking the strings rather than bowing them. As the duet ends amid a series of matching plucks, there's another standing ovation and thunderous applause. Once again Yo-Yo touches everyone he can as he exits the stage.

And now he comes back a second time as the audience roars its approval. The associate principal in the cello section cedes her seat to him. He settles in next to Joshua Roman, the symphony's 24-year-old *wunderkind* principal cello, whose mass of curly hair suggests a cartoon character who has just stuck a finger in an electric light socket. Yet there's nothing cartoonish about Roman's accomplishments. Despite youthful features suggesting that he would be carded should he go out for an after-concert drink, he became the symphony's youngest-ever principal two years ago and has already carved out a substantial career, one that like Yo-Yo's extends far beyond the concert hall and displays the same sort of stamina. Earlier this year, he—as Yo-Yo had done more than a decade before—played three concertos in a single concert. He's been to Africa. He's inspired commissions. And his resume boasts an entry that not even Yo-Yo can claim: As a teenager he was lead singer for two rock bands.

This young man appears completely at ease as he engages in a sort of mock cello duel with Yo-Yo. Their music is taken from the Sonata for Two Cellos, written by yet another French composer, Jean Barrière. Their byplay is somewhat reminiscent of the Dueling Banjos scene in the movie *Deliverance*, except that Yo-Yo and Roman are wearing tuxes and there is obviously no undercurrent of hostility. Though Roman of course lacks the long friendship with Yo-Yo that was so evident in Yo-Yo's duet with Kavafian, the two musicians interact comfortably.

When they finish, the audience is on its feet for yet another round of enthusiastic applause that subsides reluctantly.

Because not all the musicians were on stage during the concerto and the encores, there's a pause to allow them to return while minor reconfigurations are made to the seating arrangements. Then Schwarz raises his baton and—somewhat anticlimactically in view of the wildly enthusiastic reception for Yo-Yo—Ravel's *Bolero* begins, rather quietly with only a snare drum and clarinet. Very few people notice that the cello section has an additional member. Yo-Yo has quietly returned to the stage during the brief hiatus and seated himself in the last row, not doing anything to draw attention to himself.

The *Bolero* consists essentially of the same theme played over and over again, with different combinations of instruments, finally building toward a crescendo that involves all the instruments. The cellists sit idly during the first portion, and the music is certainly not the most challenging. Yet it is as if Yo-Yo has felt the excitement in the evening's performance—much of which he has generated—and wants to be a part of it for as long as he possibly can. He even turns the pages of the music for his standmates. At the conclusion, Schwarz one by one points to different orchestra members who played solo passages. Then he gestures to Yo-Yo, who seems reluctant to stand and be singled out among his fellow cello players. The evening's performance has ended.

Most of the capacity throng heads out into the warm late summer evening, happily buzzing about what they've just heard. The gala attendees remain behind. If the man who grumped about wanting to hear more Yo-Yo during the Silk Road concert in March has been in attendance, he undoubtedly will have been more than satisfied with this evening's concert.

Yo-Yo didn't have much time to relish his Seattle performance. He was due back in New York, where he would open the New York Philharmonic's season the following Tuesday, with the Dvořák concerto.

For New York music lovers who were willing to get up very early that morning—in at least one case an enthusiast even went without sleep to insure his place at the head of the line—there was a bonus: the chance to attend Yo-Yo's rehearsal with the orchestra. Two thousand free tickets to this rehearsal became available at eight o'clock that morning, and were quickly snatched up. Several hundred would-be attendees had to be turned away—not quite empty-handed, as Philharmonic officials gave each of them a discount coupon to a future concert.

The fortunate ones gave Yo-Yo and the orchestra a standing ovation when they were finished. The ovation was repeated about 12 hours later when he finished playing before the paying customers.

"Mr. Ma, who turns 52 next month, has been performing the Dvořák concerto prominently for at least 30 years," noted critic Anthony Tommasini. "But he is an artist incapable of routine. There is a fascinating convergence of qualities in his work at this stage of his great career. In a way, he plays with more maturity, breadth and insight than ever."[4]

Despite Tommasini's disclaimer, at least one aspect of Yo-Yo's performance was "routine"—and rightly so: "During the prolonged standing ovation, Mr. Ma, who always comes across as someone who thinks himself very lucky to be where he is, engaged in a hugfest with every Philharmonic player within reach."[5]

Not long after the hugfest was over, Yo-Yo was off again, this time bound for China with the Silk Road Ensemble for a four-city concert tour and a series of workshops in early October. Once again Yo-Yo was part of the opening ceremonies of the Olympics, in this case the Special Olympics in Shanghai.

"Participating in the Opening Ceremony of the Special Olympics, we are reminded that the heroes in our world come from many different places and many different walks of life,"[6] he said.

He and the Silk Road Ensemble—and the 90,000 spectators who packed Shanghai Stadium—performed an original song composed by ensemble member Osvaldo Golijov especially for the event. As they entered, spectators received a flute, which they tooted in response to signals at specified times during the group's performance.

"The 90,000 flutes sound like the Milky Way on fire," Golijov said. "China is mind-boggling and the ceremony was incredibly moving and powerful."[7]

For those keeping a mileage count, these three events alone (Seattle Symphony, New York Philharmonic, Shanghai Special Olympics) required Yo-Yo to travel almost the equivalent of one time around the world—and that was in a period of just over a month.

Early in 2008, Yo-Yo was airborne again, this time to Davos, Switzerland, for the annual meeting of the World Economic Forum. Delegates took time out from digesting the grim economic news emanating from the United States to attend ceremonies in which Yo-Yo (along with Oscar-winning actress Emma Thompson) received the organization's Crystal Award. This award recognizes the contributions of artists who have made notable efforts to increase cross-cultural contacts.

Thompson received her award first. As befits an actress who has received accolades not just for her acting but also for her writing, her acceptance speech was short but very moving. Yo-Yo then bounded up to the stage, cello in hand, and said that there was nothing he could say that could compete with her words. Instead, he announced that he would play the sarabande from one of the Bach cello suites. Despite his disclaimer, he preceded his performance with an explanation of his choice of music. The sarabande, he said, was an especially appropriate musical selection in these circumstances. It was an ideal example of cross-cultural contacts, originating in North Africa before crossing over into Spain.

In the case of the sarabande, Yo-Yo may not have gone far enough with his historical explanation. Some scholars believe that the word sarabande—and perhaps the dance itself—actually are derived from Persia. Two Persian words—serbend, or song, and sarband, or headband—are remarkably similar to the word sarabande. If there is in fact a connection, the origins of the sarabande may stretch far back in time to a part of the ancient Silk Road territory, from whence it made its way across northern Africa and eventually to Europe.

And Yo-Yo might have further entertained his audience of presidents and prime ministers, billionaires and pop icon Bono, had he told them that the original dance was considerably more ribald than the version that he played. According to one source, "The dance was a group dance mainly done by women and was considered wild in manner and a highly sexual pantomime in nature, with undulations of the body, massive hip movements, flirtations, indecent song lyrics and women using castanets."[8]

Apparently the rowdy dance upended sixteenth-century Spanish society. King Philip II of Spain, though immersed in preparations for his eventual attempt to invade England with the Spanish Armada, nonetheless took time out in 1583 to ban the sarabande. Toned down, slowed down, and cleaned up, it became considerably more upscale by the time it reached the French court in the 1600s, and Bach's corner of Germany a century later.

Music critic (and conservative columnist) Jay Nordlinger had no reservations in descending into such areas of relative irreverence. Taking note of Yo-Yo's customary physical exuberance as Forum head Klaus Schwab presented him with the award, Nordlinger noted that Yo-Yo "kisses Klaus Schwab—three times. He is an exuberant kisser and hugger, always. The late Mstislav Rostropovich was nicknamed Slava—and he was such a kisser and hugger, they further nicknamed him 'Saliva.' Yo-Yo Ma has picked up his mantle."[9]

Of course, Yo-Yo has picked up many other and far more meaningful mantles during the course of his remarkable career: Rostropovich's penchant for commissioning new music, the great hope for the survival of classical music recordings, chamber music player extraordinaire, Grammy winner, filmmaker, teacher, husband, father.

And perhaps above all, citizen of the world.

Many if not most of these can be traced to his decision to go to college when he was just 17 rather than succumb to the lure of immediately establishing a professional career.

"I just wanted to experience life," he says. "I knew that the cello that I played was totally and intimately connected to life. It's not like you get better just by practicing. You can get better by knowing the world better, figuring things out. And then having something to say."[10]

Yo-Yo Ma has always had something to say—whether a self-deprecating joke, an earnest rumination on the value of totally free and unfettered human communication, or the praise of another person. The likelihood is that his career will continue for decades, developing in yet more unexpected directions, which makes it impossible to predict which of all these "somethings" that he has to say will prove most durable and most important.

Finding out will be worth the wait.

NOTES

1. Melinda Bargreen, "Renowned Cellist Comes to Benaroya for Gala," *Seattle Times*, September 9, 2007.

2. Marina Ma, as told to John A. Rallo, *My Son, Yo-Yo* (Hong Kong, China: The Chinese University Press, 1995), p. 152.

3. Melinda Bargreen, "Exotic Instrumentation Pulls Audience In," *Seattle Times*, May 15, 2002.

4. Anthony Tommasini, "Familiar Dvorak, Redeemed with a Cellist's Many Colors," *New York Times*, September 20, 2007.

5. Ibid.

6. "Yo-Yo Ma and the Silk Road Ensemble to Tour China," World Music Central, http://worldmusiccentral.org/article.php/Yo-Yo_ma_china_tour_2007.

7. "Golijov Debuts New Composition at Special Olympics Opening Ceremony," http://www.holycross.edu/publicaffairs/features/2007–2008/golijovspecial olympics_07.

8. "StreetSwing's Dance History Archives—Sarabande Dance Page," http://www.streetswing.com/histmain/z3sarbn1.htm.

9. Jay Nordlinger, "Davos Journal, Part VII," *National Review Online*, February 1, 2008, http://article.nationalreview.com/?q=NjU2N2VhMGJhYzAxOT VlYTM2MGJiMjFlMGYzMDM2NzE=.

10. Gerri Hirshey, "We Are the World (Cellist Yo-Yo Ma)," *Parade*, January 30, 2005.

SELECTED BIBLIOGRAPHY

BOOKS

Attanas, John. *Yo-Yo Ma: A Life in Music*. Evanston, Ill.: John Gordon Burke, 2003.

Blum, David. *Quintet: Five Journeys Toward Musical Fulfillment*. Ithaca, N.Y.: Cornell University Press, 1998.

Campbell, Margaret. *The Great Cellists*. London: Victor Gallancz, 1988.

Casals, Pablo. *Joys and Sorrows: His Own Story as Told to Albert E. Kahn*. New York: Simon and Schuster, 1970.

Eisler, Edith. "Yo-Yo Ma." In *21st Century Cellists*, ed. Stacey Lynn. San Anselmo, Calif.: String Letter, 2001.

Faber, Toby. *Stradivari's Genius: Five Violins, One Cello, and Three Centuries of Enduring Perfection*. New York: Random House, 2004.

Gorin, Natalio. *Astor Piazzolla: A Memoir*. Translated, annotated, and expanded by Fernando Gonzalez. Portland, Ore.: Amadeus Press, 2001.

Hatch, Robert, and William Hatch. *The Hero Project*. New York: McGraw Hill, 2006.

Ma, Marina. *My Son, Yo-Yo*. As told to John A. Rallo. Hong Kong: The Chinese University Press, 1995.

Manchester, Karen. *The Silk Road and Beyond: Travel, Trade and Transformation*. Chicago: Art Institute of Chicago, 2007.

Pincus, Andrew L. *Musicians with a Mission: Keeping the Classical Tradition Alive*. Boston: Northeastern University Press, 2002.

Polo, Marco. *The Travels of Marco Polo*. Translated and with an introduction by Ronald Latham. New York: Penguin Books, 1958.

Prieto, Carlos. *The Adventures of a Cello*. Translated by Elena C. Murray. Austin, Tex.: Texas University Press, 2006.

ten Grotenhuis, Elizabeth, ed. *Along the Silk Road*. Seattle, Wash.: University of Washington Press, 2002.

Wood, Frances. *The Silk Road: Two Thousand Years in the Heart of Asia*. Berkeley: The University of California Press, 2002.

PERIODICALS

Abrahamson, Alan. "Winter Olympics: It's Quite a Balancing Act. Ceremony: Sept. 11 Changed Things, but Organizers Went For, and Got, a Mixture of History, Tradition and Emotion." *Los Angeles Times*, February 9, 2002.

Ax, Emanuel. "Yo-Yo Ma: Far From Charity." *New York Times*, August 15, 1999.

Alexander, Vinita M. "Living Legend." *The Harvard Crimson*, May 7, 2004.

Bargreen, Melinda. "The Silk Road Project: It's Smooth, Heavenly and Engaging." *Seattle Times*, May 14, 2002.

———. "Renowned Cellist Comes to Benaroya for Gala." *Seattle Times*, September 9, 2007.

Burstein, Nathan. "Following the Silk Road to Tel Aviv." *Jerusalem Post*, May 24, 2006.

Carton, Barbara. "Boston Tries to Revamp City Hall Plaza." *Wall Street Journal*, January 28, 2001.

Chang, Tahlin. "Cross Over, Beethoven." *Newsweek*, April 20, 1998.

Chase, Stephanie. "Yo-Yo Ma: A 'Retrofitted' Cello." *New York Times*, September 5, 1999.

Covington, Richard. "Yo-Yo Ma's Other Passion." *Smithsonian Magazine*, June, 2002.

Cutts, Paul. "Caravans in the Desert." *The Guardian*, September 7, 2007.

Davidson, Justin. "Have Cello, Will Travel: For the Tireless Yo-Yo Ma, All the World's an Audience." *Newsday*, November 30, 1997.

———. "Score One for Bach: The Music Transcends Yo-Yo Ma's New Film." *Newsday*, April 1, 1998.

DeLatiner, Barbara. "A Love of Music Inspires a Crusade." *New York Times*, April 26, 1998.

Dolgonos, Sarah A., and Amit R. Paley. "College Taught Ma to Play His Own Tune." *Harvard Crimson*, June 5, 2001.

Duchen, Jessica. "Still Striking a Chord." *The Independent*, January 7, 2005.

Dulak, Michelle. "Dipping a Toe into the Early-Music Waters." *New York Times*, August 1, 1999.

Dyer, Richard. "Ma and McFerrin: A Match Made in Tanglewood." *Boston Globe*, January 19, 1991.

———. "Odd Couples: As Record Companies Strive to Match the Success of the Three Tenors Album, They Offer Celebrity Pairings that Range from the Memorable to the Purely Commercial." *Boston Globe*, March 15, 1992.

Eisenberg, Evan. "Music: Through College and Life, in Harmony." *New York Times*, July 15, 2001.

Eisler, Edith. "A Dynamic Duo on Their Silver Anniversary." *Andante* (March 2001).

———. "Continuity in Diversity." *Strings* (May/June 2001).

———. "The Music Doctor: Yeou-Cheng Ma's Double Career." *Strings* (March/April 1995).

———. "Yo-Yo Ma: Music from the Soul." *Strings* (May/June 1992).

———. "Yo-Yo Ma and the Silk Road Project." *Andante*, April 2001.

Elliot, Dorinda. "A Conversation with Yo-Yo Ma." *Conde Nast Traveler* (May 2007).

Finkelstein, Katherine E. "In Concert, Searchers Retrieve Yo-Yo Ma's Lost Stradivarius [sic]." *New York Times*, October 17, 1999.

Fleming, John. "Selling Yo-Yo Ma to the Masses." *St. Petersburg Times*, October 31, 2004.

Gardiner, Beth. "Yo-Yo Ma Forgets Cello in Cab, but Cops Get It Back." *South Coast Today*, October 17, 1999.

Ginell, Richard S. "Yo-Yo Ma: Inspired by Bach Review." *Variety*, April 1, 1998.

Goddard, Peter. "Yo-Yo Ma: 'I'm Not Thinking of Mortality . . . but I Am Thinking of the Inner Life, where Music Exists.' " *Toronto Star*, January 6, 1996.

Goodman, Walter. "Television Review: Cellist Finds Accompanists for J. S. Bach." *New York Times*, April 1, 1998.

Handy, Bruce, and Daniel S. Levy. "Yo-Yo Ma's Suite Life?" *Time*, March 23, 1998.

Hirshey, Gerri. "We Are the World (Cellist Yo-Yo Ma)." *Parade*, January 30, 2005.

Holden, Stephen. "Grappelli, 80, Stars at His Tribute." *New York Times*, April 16, 1988.

Holland, Bernard. "Music Review; Yo-Yo Ma Looks Back, With His Cello." *New York Times*, February 23, 1999.

———. "Review/Cello: Yo-Yo Ma Personalizes Six Bach Suites." *New York Times*, January 15, 1991.

———. "When a Virtuoso and His Cello Take to the Road." *New York Times*, May 24, 1981.

Horowitz, Joseph. "Exuberance Plus Serenity Equals Yo-Yo Ma." *New York Times*, April 15, 1979.

James, Jamie. "Yo-Yo Ma May Be a National Institution, but He Continues to Reinvent Himself." *New York Times*, December 31, 1995.

Kosman, Joshua. "35 Who Made a Difference: Yo-Yo Ma." *Smithsonian* (November 2005).

Kozinn, Allan. "A Benefactor Tells Why He Did It." *New York Times*, March 2, 1986.

———. "A Once Proud Industry Fends Off Extinction." *New York Times*, December 8, 1996.

———. "Music Review; A Program Angry, Lyrical and Wacky." *New York Times*, March 8, 2003.

McKeough, Kevin. "An American Odyssey." *Strings* (May/June 2002).

Miller, Jake. "Travelers on the Silk Road: 2006." *Yoga + Joyful Living* (September/October 2006).

Oestreich, James. "Making a 1712 Cello Sound Less Modern." *New York Times*, February 20, 1999.

Page, Tim. "Leonard Rose Benefit." *New York Times*, November 1, 1986.

———. "Ma and Ax: A Special Blend of Cello and Piano." *New York Times*, November 16, 1984.

Perez-Franco, Roberto. "CD Review: An Experiment in Musical, Cultural Fusion—Yo-Yo Ma's Latest CD Tells the Story of Asia's Silk Road." *The Tech*, November 30, 2007.

Reynolds, Christopher. "Winter Olympics: The Music Isn't Live, Either. Olympics: Cold Weather and a Global Audience Require Performers to Try to Match Recordings during the Opening and Closing Ceremonies." *Los Angeles Times*, February 23, 2002.

Rothstein, Edward. "Review/Music: Yo-Yo Ma and His New 'Hyper' Cello." *New York Times*, August 17, 1991.

Rubinstein, Leslie. "Oriental Musicians Come of Age." *New York Times*, November 23, 1980.

Ryan, Tim. "Yo! Cellist Extraordinaire Yo-Yo Ma Reveals His Secret to Balance in His Life." *Honolulu Star-Bulletin*, March 16, 1999.

Sachs, Andrea. "The Downside of Being a Child Prodigy." *Time*, September 6, 2006.

Scherman, Tony. "Music: Fiddling While the Old Barriers Burn." *New York Times*, April 2, 2000.

Schonberg, Harold C. "In the East Room, Horowitz and 2 Surprises." *New York Times*, October 6, 1986.

Siegel, Ed. "Playing the Full Human Range: Yo-Yo Ma Plays the Cello to Create a Portrait of the Artist." *Boston Globe*, August 6, 1995.

"Silk Road Chicago Ends with Collaborative Fable Featuring Yo Yo Ma and School Children." *International Herald Tribune*, June 1, 2007.

Smith, Ken. "Setting Off on the Silk Road (Project)." *Andante*, September 2001.

Steinberg, Martin. "Yo-Yo Ma Will Take Silk Road to China." Associated Press, September 26, 2007.

Tommasini, Anthony. "A Cellist Continually in Search of an Author." *New York Times*, March 26, 1995.

———. "Familiar Dvorak, Redeemed with a Cellist's Many Colors." *New York Times*, September 20, 2007.

———. "Music Review; A Concert Offers City Some Time for Healing." *New York Times*, October 1, 2001.

Tyrangiel, Josh. "10 Questions for Yo-Yo Ma." *Time*, March 27, 2005.

Watrous, Peter. "Grappelli at Carnegie Hall, Still Seeking New Options." *New York Times*, October 8, 1989.

Wilson, Elizabeth. "Forever Young." *BBC Music Magazine*, February 2005.

———. "Civilization's Retreat." *Time*, June 27, 1940.

———. "Yo-Yo's Way with the Strings." *Time*, January 19, 1981.

WEBSITES

Authored Articles

Covington, Richard. "Mark Morris Interview." http://www.salon.com/weekly/interview2960909.html.

Dryden, Ken. "Stéphane Grappelli—Discography: Anything Goes, with Yo-Yo Ma." All Music Guide. http://www.legacyrecordings.com/Stephane-Grappelli-with-Yo-Yo-Ma/Anything-Goes-The-Music-of-Cole-Porter.aspx.

Eisler, Edith. "Yo-Yo Ma: Solo." http://www.amazon.ca/Solo-Mark-OConnor/dp/B00000K4II7.

Janof, Tim. "Leonard Rose Remembered." http://www.cello.org/Newsletter/Articles/rose/rose.htm.

Jesseson, Robert. "The Etymology of the Words 'Violin' and 'Violoncello': Implications on Literature in the Early History of the Cello." http://www.cello.org/Newsletter/Articles/celloetymology.htm.

Jong, Mabel. "Yo-Yo Ma: Family Is Best Investment." http://www.bankrate.com/brm/news/investing/20030821a1.asp.

Keller, Johanna. "2003: New Challenges for the Performing Arts: Thirteen Ways of Looking at the Future." http://www.musicalamerica.com/features/?fid=88&fyear=2003.

Kirshnit, Frederick L. "Instruments of Mass Seduction—Part I: The Cello." ConcertoNet.com—the Classical Music Network. http://www.concertonet. com/scripts/edito.php?ID_edito=60.

Ma, Yo-Yo. "The Silk Road Project—Vision." http://www.silkroadproject.org/ about/vision.html.

Machover, Todd. "'Classic' Hyper instruments 1986–1992: A Composer's Approach to the Evolution of Intelligent Musical Instruments." http:// brainop.media.mit.edu/Archive/Hyperinstruments/classichyper.html.

Nickson, Chris. "Silk Road Journeys: When Strangers Meet." All Music Guide. http://www.billboard.com/bbcom/discography/more.jsp?tp=albums&pid= 9122&aid=531035.

Nordlinger, Jay. "Davos Journal, Part VII." *National Review Online*, February 1, 2008. http://article.nationalreview.com/?q=NjU2N2VhMGJhYzAxOTVl YTM2MGJiMjFlMGYzMDM2NzE=.

Osmond, Susan. "Yo-Yo Ma's Silk Road Project." TheWorld&I.com. http://www. worldandi.com/public/2002/april/silkintro.html.

Sanders, Linda. "Music Capsule Review: Hush; Play (1992)." *Entertainment Weekly*, March 6, 1992. http://www.ew.com/ew/article/0,,309794,00.html.

Saslav, Isidor. "The Day Of The 'Cello." http://www.swans.com/library/art13/ saslav02.html.

Selberg, Ryan. *Internet Cello Society Newsletter*, March/April 2002. http://cello. org/Newsletter/marapr02.htm.

Tassel, Janet. "Yo-Yo Ma's Journeys." *Harvard Magazine* (March/April 2000). http://harvardmagazine.com/2000/03/yo-yo-mas-journeys.html.

Widran, Jonathan. "Obrigado Brazil—Live in Concert: Critic's Review." *All Music Guide*. http://music.msn.com/album/?album=32405621&menu=review.

Yanowitch, Lee. "French Jazz Violinist Stephane Grappelli Dead At 89." http:// www.cyberbites.com/marleys_ghost/grappelliobit.html.

Unauthored Articles

"Albert Schweitzer Biography." http://nobelprize.org/nobel_prizes/peace/laure ates/1952/schweitzer-bio.html.

"Albert Schweitzer Fellowship." http://www.schweitzerfellowship.org/.

"Annan Appoints Cellist Yo-Yo Ma as UN Peace Messenger for His Music of Harmony." http://www.un.org/apps/news/story.asp?NewsID=19941&Cr= messenger&Cr1=peace.

"Antonio Meneses: Bach Cello Suites." http://magnatune.com/artists/meneses.

"Arts First: An Evening with Yo-Yo Ma." http://athome.harvard.edu/dh/yym. html.

"Astor Piazzolla—Bandoneón Concerto." http://www.laphil.com/music/piece_ detail.cfm?id=1091.

"Baroque Composers and Musicians: Johann Sebastian Bach." http://classicalmu
    sic.about.com/gi/dynamic/offsite.htm?zi=1/XJ&sdn=classicalmusic&cdn
    =entertainment&tm=60&gps=36_65_1072_855&f=20&su=p284.9.336.
    ip_&tt=11&bt=1&bts=1&zu=http%3A//www.baroquemusic.org/bqxjs
    bach.html.

"Basic Black: A Conversation and Performance with Esperanza Spalding." http://
    www.wgbh.org/schedules/program-info?program_id=25065&episode_
    id=3114218.

"Begin Again Again." http://web.media.mit.edu/~tod/Tod/begin.html.

"Bright Sheng." http://www.schirmer.com/default.aspx?TabId=2419&State_2872=
    2&ComposerId_2872=1436.

"Bright Sheng—The Song and Dance of Tears." http://www.schirmer.com/
    Default.aspx?TabId=2420&State_2874=2&workId_2874=32935.

"The Davydov Strad." http://www.cello.org/heaven/masters/davydov.htm.

"Director's Statement—Atom Egoyan." http://www.sonyclassical.com/releases/
    63203/films.html.

"Director's Statement—Barbara Willis Sweete." http://www.sonyclassical.com/
    releases/63203/films.html.

"Director's Statement—Patricia Rozema." http://www.sonyclassical.com/releases/
    63203/films.html.

"Fred McFeely Rogers: 2002 Commencement Address at Dartmouth College."
    http://www.indigo.org/mrrogers.html.

"From the Top: Live from Carnegie Hall, April 3, 2007." http://www.carnegie
    hall.org/article/newsletter/art_newsletter_07040301.html#fromthetop#fr
    omthetop.

"From the Top: Radio and Television: Hall of Fame—Yo-Yo Ma." http://www.
    fromthetop.org/Programs/HallOfFame.cfm?pid=1858.

"Giovanni Piranesi." http://www.artchive.com/artchive/P/piranesi.html.

"Golijov Debuts New Composition at Special Olympics Opening Ceremony."
    http://www.holycross.edu/publicaffairs/features/2007–2008/golijovspe
    cialolympics_07.

"Jean-Pierre Rampal." http://www.nfaonline.org/resMuseum7.asp.

"Johann Pachelbel's Canon in D major and Popular Culture." http://www.origen
    music.com/canon-pachelbel2.html.

"The Library of Congress presents . . . Musician Biographies: Yo-Yo Ma, Cel-
    list." http://lcweb2.loc.gov/diglib/ihas/html/greatconversations/great-bios-
    ma.html#disco

"Mark Morris Dance Group." http://markmorrisdancegroup.org.

"Meet the Composer—The Insider's Scoop, Lillian & Maurice Barbash." http://
    www.meetthecomposer.org/indguide/barbash.html.

"Messengers of Peace." http://www.un.org/News/ossg/factmess.htm.

"Mr. Rogers' Passion for Learning." http://www.aarp.org/nrta/Articles/a2002–12–19-nrta_rogers.html.

"Music Garden." http://www.aviewoncities.com/toronto/musicgarden.htm.

"The Silk Road Project Adds Concerts in Dallas and Atlanta." http://www.silk roadproject.org/press/releases/011010.html.

"Six French Interviews with Mstislav Rostropovich, November 2005 to November 2006." Translated by David Abrams. http://www.cello.org/Newsletter/Articles/rostrofrench/rostrofrench.htm.

"Stephen Albert—Cello Concerto." http://209.218.170.3/composers/albert_cello_concerto.html.

"StreetSwing's Dance History Archives—Sarabande Dance Page." http://www.streetswing.com/histmain/z3sarbn1.htm.

"The World's Best and Worst Parks." http://www.pps.org/info/newsletter/september2004/september2004_best_worst.

"Yo-Yo Ma and the Silk Road Ensemble to Tour China." http://worldmusiccentral.org/article.php/Yo-Yo_ma_china_tour_2007.

"Yo-Yo Ma: Earth's Most Charming Male?" *Goldsea Asian American Daily*, May 26, 2004. http://goldsea.com/Air/Issues/Ma/ma.html.

"Yo-Yo Ma Has Been Named *Billboard*'s 'Classical Artist of the Year.'" http://www.sonyclassical.com/news/awards_top.htm.

OTHER SOURCES

Heidi Lehwalder, personal interview with the author, February 19, 2008.

Inspired by Bach. Filmed by Rhombus Media, Toronto, Canada. Producer: Niv Fichman. 1997. The six films of this series are here presented in the chronological order in which they were filmed.

The Music Garden. Director: Kevin McMahon. Cast: Yo-Yo Ma, Julie Moir Messervy.

The Sound Of The Carceri. Director: Francois Girard. Cast: Yo-Yo Ma, Steven Epstein.

Falling Down Stairs. Director: Barbara Willis Sweete. Choreographer: Mark Morris. Cast: Yo-Yo Ma, Mark Morris, Mark Morris Dance Group.

Sarabande. Director-writer: Atom Egoyan. Cast: Yo-Yo Ma, Lori Singer, Don McKellar, Arsinee Khanjian, George Sperdakos, Jan Rube, David Hemblen, Tracy Wright, Rod Wilson, Johnnie Eisen, Calvin Green, Sam Malkin, Vernon Regeher.

Struggle For Hope. Director: Niv Fichman. Choreographer: Tamasaburo Bando. Cast: Yo-Yo Ma, Tamasaburo Bando.

Six Gestures. Director-Writer: Patricia Rozema. Cast: Yo-Yo Ma, Jayne Torvill, Christopher Dean, Tom McCamus, Mark Kinney, Baby Dee, Niv Fichman, Chris Farr, Jacoba Rozema, Karen Kenedy, Heinar Piller.

"Interview: Cellist Yo-Yo Ma on His Music and New CD." *Weekend Edition Saturday*, National Public Radio, May 25, 2002.

Kassia Sing, personal interview with the author, May 23, 2007.

INDEX

About the Author

JIM WHITING is a professional writer, editor, and photographer and the author of more than 100 books, chiefly nonfiction works written for children. For 17 years he published *Northwest Runner* magazine, a monthly publication. He frequently has written about music and is the author of 15 biographies of classical and modern composers in the Masters of Music series for young readers from Mitchell Lane. His Web site is www.Jim Whiting.com.